W9-BZA-944

TWENTY
THOUSAND LEAGUES
UNDER THE SEA

AN ADAPTED CLASSIC

TWENTY THOUSAND LEAGUES UNDER THE SEA

JULES VERNE

GLOBE FEARON

Pearson Learning Group

ARDIS EDWARDS BURTON

formerly with the Department of English
John Sweet Union High School
Crockett, California

M. JERRY WEISS

Distinguished Service Professor of Communication
Jersey City State College
Jersey City, New Jersey

Cover design: Marek Antoniak
Cover illustration: Alan Nahigian

Copyright © 1995 by Pearson Education, Inc., publishing as Globe Fearon®, an imprint of Pearson Learning Group, 299 Jefferson Road, Parsippany, NJ 07054. All rights reserved. No part of this book may be reproduced or transmitted in any form or by any means, electronic, or mechanical, including photocopying, recording, or by any information storage and retrieval system, without permission in writing from the publisher. For information regarding permission(s), write to Rights and Permissions Department.

ISBN 0-835-90217-X
Printed in the United States of America

13 14   08 09

Globe
Fearon

Pearson Learning Group

1-800-321-3106
www.pearsonlearning.com

ABOUT THE AUTHOR

Jules Verne was born in France in 1828. He was one of the first writers of what is now called science fiction. He was always writing of the future. Verne wrote about submarines, television, helicopters, movies, airplanes, and spaceships before they were really invented.

He was not a scientist, a sailor, nor a submarine builder. All he knew about science and the sea was what he read or imagined. As a boy, he ran away to sea. But the ship's captain sent for Jules' father, who took him home. Jules promised that he would do all of his traveling by reading and writing in the future.

Some of Jules Verne's other books include: *A Journey to the Center of the Earth, From the Earth to the Moon, Around the World in Eighty Days,* and *The Mysterious Island.*

Jules Verne died in France in 1905.

PREFACE

Before submarines were invented, they were imagined. It took hundreds of years for the impossible to come true. But people finally made a ship that could move under water. It took years to solve the problems of supplying air, keeping water out, rising and sinking, and seeing where to go. But Jules Verne imagined ways to solve all of these problems in *Twenty Thousand Leagues Under the Sea.* This is the story of the amazing submarine, *The Nautilus,* launched by Captain Nemo over 100 years ago.

Many of the things in this book are common today. But when the book was written, they were only visions of the future. In the following pages you will meet the captain, crew, and passengers of *The Nautilus.* You will share their long and exciting adventure under the sea. You will read about monsters, sunken treasure, and wonders of the deep. And you will see that many of the captain's inventions are being used today. Many of his inventions, however, are still only imagined.

ADAPTER'S NOTE

In preparing this edition of *Twenty Thousand Leagues Under the Sea,* Jules Verne's main purpose has been kept in mind. Since the book was originally published, however, language has changed. We have modified or omitted some passages and some vocabulary. We have, however, kept as much of the original as possible.

CONTENTS

PART I

PART II

TWENTY THOUSAND LEAGUES UNDER THE SEA

Part 1

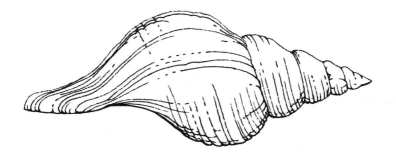

1 Is It a Monster?

"What do you think we're looking for, anyway?" asked the first sailor. "A whale?"

"Of course!" answered the other. "What else?"

Several of us were aloft in the masts and rigging of our ship. All of us were gazing steadily at the vast Atlantic. The sailors were talking.

I listened to them, looking from one to another as they talked. Sitting on a crosstree, I watched the sea too, holding on to the mast.

"I think it's a whale we're after," spoke up a bearded sailor. "Or maybe a sea monster."

For several months there had been a great mystery. People talked of little else. Many ships at sea had seen a huge object larger than a whale. It could move much faster than a whale, and sometimes it seemed to glow. No one knew what it was.

No one made us sit in the crosstrees; it was an uncomfortable perch. But we wanted to sit there for we were excited. We watched the bright sea eagerly, as the ship rocked gently.

"Well, whatever it is, I'd like to see it!" spoke up the cabin boy. He was barely fifteen years old. "I've looked long and hard. Sometimes I think my head will fall off."

"Wouldn't I like to see it harpooned!" said the bearded man. "What a sight that would be!"

"And chasing him down—wouldn't that be fun?" said another sailor.

"As for me, I'd like to see it hoisted aboard," said another. "I'd like to help kill it. That would suit me!"

All the men were excited.

"Well, I'd be satisfied just to see it," said the cabin boy again, never taking his eyes off the sea. "Then I'd win Captain Farragut's prize. Just think! Two thousand dollars goes to the first person who sees it! Even if he's a cabin boy, he gets the money."

For some time the men were silent. Each was busy with his own thoughts. Each one was thinking of how he would spend the $2,000.

"Some people say it's not an animal at all," spoke up one sailor. "They say it's a floating island, or an uncharted rock. Some think it is a sunken wreck."

"Then it must have a machine in its stomach— that's all I can say," the Portuguese sailor answered him. "It changes positions so fast, and it spouts water 150 feet into the air."

"Yes, it spouts water!" shouted another. "If that isn't a whale, then what is it?"

Then up spoke Ned Land. Ned was the harpooner of our ship, the *Abraham Lincoln*.

"Are you men crazy?" he said. "How can you believe such nonsense? You are all seafaring men. You know there are no such monsters in the sea!"

"Then you don't think it's an animal?" asked the cabin boy. He was disappointed, I thought.

"Why, the biggest whale ever caught was only 50 or 60 yards long," answered Ned. "But this thing is 300 feet long! And you've never seen such a thing as a sea monster!"

I could see that Ned Land was no ordinary sailor. He was a Canadian of about forty. He was more than six feet tall, and a powerful fellow. He was smart and bold. Everyone listened to Ned Land: they wanted to hear what he thought about this mystery of the sea.

Ned Land was the king of harpooners of the whole world. Captain Farragut did well to get him for our voyage.

"Now don't you be too sure, Ned Land," said one of the sailors. "We don't know what is in the sea. No one has ever seen all the strange creatures that live down there in the dark waters. There are monsters, no doubt, bigger than any that have ever been seen."

Ned Land was silent. He didn't believe this, it was plain.

"Do you know what I think?" said the cabin boy. "I think it's a narwhal,[1] a sea animal ten times bigger than any whale. A sea-unicorn—that's what I think it is."

---

[1] Narwhal—an arctic whale about 24 feet long including the tusk, which resembles a unicorn's.

The others nodded. Except for Ned Land, everyone agreed with him.

"Ned, you are a whaler," spoke another sailor. "You know that there are huge whales in the sea."

"Of course there are. I know that," answered Ned. "For thirty years, man and boy, I've followed the sea. I've chased many a whale in my time. I've killed a lot of them. But I never saw one that could damage an iron ship."

"But Ned, a narwhal could!" said the cabin boy. "I've heard of whaling ships that the tusk of a narwhal pierced through."

"Wooden ships, maybe," answered Ned, "though I never saw it done. But not iron ships. Whatever this thing is, it went through iron-plate nearly two inches thick. No narwhal could do that!"

"But a narwhal has a tusk seven or eight feet long," said the bearded man.

"What if it does?" answered Ned. "Suppose a narwhal were ten times stronger. Suppose it had a tusk six times longer. I still don't think it could make a hole in iron-plate. And draw back again, men! Remember that! The tusk wasn't just buried in the ship and left there. Whatever struck those ships, withdrew again!"

"Yes, but the United States government equipped this ship," said the cabin boy. I could see that he was a clever boy, for his age. "The United States government sent us out on this search. We are supposed to find the narwhal and kill it. So the United States government thinks it is a narwhal."

It was true. The United States government had fitted out our ship. We had every kind of harpoon. We had hand harpoons. We had harpoons thrown by a gun.

We even had the newest American whaling gun. It could throw a nine-pound shell ten miles.

But best of all, we had Ned Land. He had no equal in his dangerous job.

An hour or more had passed. I had not said a word, for none of the men knew me. I had listened to their talk because it interested me. I wanted to hear all of their arguments. It was plain what they thought: they all believed that the *Abraham Lincoln* was chasing a huge narwhal. Captain Farragut thought so, too. **But Ned** Land didn't know. He was not sure.

"Well, I'm still not sure it's an animal," said Ned Land. "I'm just not sure. You'll have to prove it to me."

I made up my mind to talk further with Ned Land. I wanted to know him. I admired people who didn't make up their minds too fast.

2 I Talked With Ned Land

Next morning I found Ned sitting at the stern, watching the sea. He was mending a rope. The sun was bright and warm on my shoulders. On the sea, waves were dancing.

We were three weeks out of New York, heading due south. Before long we would round the tip of South America. In a week we would be in the Pacific Ocean, where the mysterious creature of the sea had last been sighted.

"Well, Ned," I said to him, "do you still refuse to believe that we are looking for a huge whale?"

"I wouldn't say that, sir," he replied. "But I am not stupid, even if I am just a sailor. Why should I believe in sea monsters? You don't."

Ned had a friendly smile. I liked him at once.

Ned and I are old friends now; we have been good friends for many years. We have talked for whole days at a time. I wish I could live a hundred years, so I could write down all the good stories Ned has told me. But we liked each other right away.

"You are a scientist, sir?" he asked me.

"Yes," I answered. "That is, a science teacher. The American government sent me on this trip. It is a great opportunity for me, for I will study undersea plants and animals. By the way, Ned, just call me Pierre."

I could not think of his calling me *sir*, when I was years younger than he.

"Then you know about this great mystery of the sea? I thought only seafaring men knew about that."

"Everyone knows about it," I told him. "People all over the world are talking about it. Newspapers print stories about it every day in Paris, London, and New York. Even scientists are talking about it."

"The scientists? What do they think it is?"

"Oh, some of them laugh and joke about it," I told him.

"Well, it isn't a joke, even if they do laugh about it," he said seriously.

"Everybody doesn't joke about it, Ned," I told him. "I don't, and I am a scientist. The United States government doesn't joke about it. They sent me on this trip. The governments of England and France don't joke about it. Germany, Spain, Russia, and Italy—they don't joke about it. Even Turkey has studied it."

"I didn't know that," said Ned. "What kind of science are you interested in?"

"I am supposed to know all about undersea life and animals. I have written two books on the subject."

"Well, then you ought to know what this thing is. Do you think it is a floating island? A sunken wreck? An animal? Or what?"

"That is a hard question, so I can't give you an easy answer. Perhaps I'd better tell you what I don't think."

"Tell me what you don't think, then," he said, clearing a place for me to sit.

"First, I don't think it's a floating island or a coral reef or a sunken wreck. It's been seen in too many places, and the places are too far apart. And it seems to move pretty fast, under its own power." Ned was watching me closely.

"Next, I don't think it's just a dream, or imagination," I said.

"Well, people do imagine sea monsters. The sea is a mysterious place, sad and lonely. People get to imagining things. Then you think it is an animal?"

"I didn't say that," I told him. "But if it were an animal, how could it stand the pressure of the deep sea without being crushed?"

"That's right. The pressure must be very great down there," he said.

"Six miles down, the pressure is hundreds of billions of pounds per square inch."

"The devil it is!" he exclaimed. "Why, to stand such pressure, an animal must be built with steel plates eight or ten inches thick all over it!"

"Exactly!" I said. "Now, can you imagine such a huge animal as that, with steel plates eight or ten inches thick?"

"Whew!" he whistled, "it's even worse than I thought!"

"Now, just think of the damage such an animal could cause. Suppose it is 300 feet long, as they say."

"And suppose it is going faster than any ship, as they say?" he broke in.

"And suppose," I went on, "that it came full speed against the hull of a ship. What would it do to the ship? Remember, it has steel plates several inches thick."

"Why, it would wreck any ship that sails," he said.

"Well, Ned, all I can say is this. If it is an animal, then it has to be like the one we described."

"There just can't be an animal that big, Pierre. There just can't be an animal that strong, covered with armor-plate eight inches thick. What on earth can it be?"

Ned picked up his rope. His strong hands untwisted it as he talked. He frowned.

"There's just one more possibility, as I see it," I told him. "It could be a submarine of some kind—a huge, powerful submarine."

"You mean a ship that sails underwater? Who would build it?"

"That's exactly the question," I said. "I don't think it's likely myself. One person couldn't possibly build it all alone. One person couldn't operate it all alone. Perhaps some state or country might build such a thing; I don't know. These are troubled times all over the world."

"But where would they build it?" Ned asked. "And when? How?"

"That's just it. Countries all have spies that watch one another. If any country built such a submarine, all the other countries would know about it. No one could keep such a secret. That would be impossible!"

"Would it?" he asked. "I wonder. I just wonder."

3   *Three Months Go By*

Day after day went by, and not much happened.

We sailed around the tip of South America and headed northwest into the Pacific Ocean. We still watched the ocean day and night. I didn't care much about the prize money, but I caught the fever of excitement from the other men.

We went to our meals and took a few hours to sleep. We did our work. But rain or shine, we watched the sea.

Sometimes I leaned on the rail, sometimes I climbed up in the rigging. Sometimes I sat on the prow —always looking. So did all the other men. My eyes ached from the sun, and I was as brown as copper.

At night I lived to see Crux Australis, or The Southern Cross, the most interesting and beautiful constellation in the Southern Hemisphere. All sailors love it. In the daytime I would watch with the other men.

Weeks went by this way, for the weather was still good. We saw many ships. We asked if they had seen the narwhal, but no one had seen it.

On July 27 we crossed the equator again, headed for the North Pacific, where the mysterious sea creature had last been seen.

By and by we were near Japan. We were all so excited now that we could hardly eat or sleep. Twenty times a day there was a false alarm. We would all rush to the rail and strain our eyes. But it was never the narwhal.

Three months went by this way, then the excitement began to wear off. We were tired and bored. We no longer had any hope. We were ready to give up. Not one of us cared about the whale any longer; all we wanted was to turn around and go home. There was nothing else to do.

There was no mutiny on board. We had simply done our best without success. It was not our fault that we saw no narwhal. Finally, on November 2, we asked Captain Farragut to go back to America.

Captain Farragut called us all up on the deck, where he stood facing us.

"My men," he said, "you have been wonderful! I have never seen such courage and determination. I never saw such a splendid crew. If the narwhal had been near us, you would have seen it. Faithfully you have watched, night and day."

The men answered with a cheer. They liked his praise.

"But you are right," he went on, "there is nothing to do but turn back. We might as well admit it. Maybe there is no such animal. If there is, it is not in these waters, or we would have seen it. Now it is wise to turn back to New York."

Now the men cheered wildly. They were very happy.

"But wait, men, and listen. Once Columbus was in charge of three ships that were looking for a new route to India. They sailed for many weeks, until the men gave up and wanted to turn back. But Columbus begged them to go on for just three more days. They did—and they discovered America!"

The men were silent. They were all thinking, and they knew he was right.

"That is what I am asking you, my brave men— just three more days. How does that strike you? I give you my word of honor, as captain of this ship: if we do not see the monster in three days, we will turn back."

Now the men began to talk it over. They liked Captain Farragut. He was fair with them. He was a brave man, and he hated to give up. So they agreed to go on for three more days.

After that we all felt better. We fell to our work with a will. We watched as hard as ever, and the first day went by in good spirit. But we saw no monster.

The second day the ship went more slowly. But still there was no sign of the monster.

Night was coming on. It was eight bells. Clouds covered the moon and the sea rocked gently. Waves slapped the sides of the ship softly. By noon next day our time would be up. Captain Farragut would then turn back, leaving the South Pacific. We would head back south, the way we had come. The coast of Japan was now only two hundred miles away.

I was leaning over the starboard side. The crew was in the ratlines watching the sea.

"Well, this is your last chance to win the $2,000," I said to Ned, who was leaning over the rail as I walked up.

"There isn't going to be any prize," he said gloomily. "If the prize were a million dollars, nobody would win it."

"Come now," I said, "this is exciting! Look at all the men. This is our last night. Tomorrow we will be headed back to New York."

"But why get all excited?" he said. "This whole trip was a wild-goose chase. In the first place, there isn't any monster. In the second place, we are unlucky. It has all been a complete waste of time."

"A waste of time! Not for me!" I told him. "I think it has been great. I never had more fun in my life!"

"Fun? Is it fun to make a fool out of yourself? That is what we have done. Other people will have fun too —laughing at us. They will—"

He did not finish his sentence.

"Look out! There it is! I see it!" He pointed over my shoulder.

4 Ned Land Wins the Prize

The whole crew ran toward Ned Land. Captain, officers, sailors, cabin boy, engineers, stokers—everyone ran to his side.

"There it is!" he pointed. It was so dark that I wondered how he could see anything at all. But he was not mistaken. There it was!

True enough, there was the monster, about 200 yards away. It was 10 or 20 feet under the water, throwing off a strange light. The light was in the shape of a large pointed oval, very long. It was moving, first forward, then backward. Then it came toward us.

"Reverse the engines!" roared Captain Farragut. The *Abraham Lincoln* made a semicircle. "Now, go ahead!"

The animal sailed around our ship. Then it moved away two or three miles, leaving a phosphorescent track. Suddenly it rushed toward us.

About twenty feet away, it suddenly stopped, slid under our hull, and came up on the other side. Then it fled.

We gasped. Captain Farragut swore. Why didn't the monster attack us?

"There is no doubt now," Captain Farragut said. "We have a huge narwhal all right. And it is electric besides. This is the most terrible monster in the sea!"

We stayed up all night. No one thought of sleep. We cut down our speed, but the narwhal did not leave.

17

About midnight its light died out, like a huge glow-worm. But we could hear it all night, pounding like a 2,000-horsepower engine.

"There it is again!" cried Ned Land before daylight. I was beside him. Two jets of steam and water spouted to the height of 120 feet. I still thought it was a whale spouting.

"Full steam ahead!" shouted Farragut.

The *Abraham Lincoln* headed straight for the monster. It darted away. For nearly an hour we chased it. We could, however, get nowhere near it.

"We shall not take this cursed beast easily," said the bearded sailor.

"Put on more steam!" ordered the captain.

The *Abraham Lincoln* was the fastest ship in the American navy. But the animal went at the same speed. We could not gain a foot.

"More steam!" yelled the captain. "Full steam ahead!"

"That's all we have, sir," answered the engineer.

The animal was just loafing along, playing with us. We could not catch it. We couldn't even get near it.

What a chase! I cannot tell you how excited we were. We leaned over the rail, shouting until we were hoarse. You would have thought we were crazy men.

Ned Land stayed right at his post, harpoon in hand. Just as he was ready to shoot, however, the animal would move out of range. It was a wild morning.

Noon came, but we were no nearer.

"Shoot the beast!" ordered Captain Farragut.

Ah, that was it! Guns were loaded and swung around into firing position. The men aimed carefully. They fired. The first bullet overshot the animal. The second shot was a hit, but the bullet slid off the rounded surface of the whale.

Then the chase began again.

"I'll catch that beast, if I blow up the ship!" swore the captain.

We must have sailed three hundred miles that day. Round and round we went. When night came on, we were no nearer the sea creature. Then darkness fell and we lost sight of it.

About eleven we saw its lights again, shining dimly three miles or so away. It was not moving.

"Many a whale has been killed in its sleep," said Ned Land. "Let's slip up on it while it is asleep!"

Captain Farragut thought that was a good idea. He gave orders to attack the whale in its sleep. Ned went to his place under the bowsprit, harpoon in hand.

Slowly, and with motors throbbing quietly, we moved closer. Not a word was spoken. We could hardly breathe. Now we were 200 yards away from the lights. Then we were only 100 feet away.

I saw Ned Land at this moment. He leaned forward, rope in one hand and harpoon in the other. It was a marvelous picture he made. The animal was barely twenty feet away.

Suddenly Ned's arm straightened. The harpoon whistled through the air. I heard it strike.

The lights suddenly went out. Two huge spouts of water from the enemy then flooded the *Abraham Lincoln* under the half-moon. A deluge of water rushed completely over our decks. It knocked men off their feet. It washed everything loose on deck into the sea. I frantically grabbed for something to hang onto, but there was nothing. In a flash I went overboard. I pitched headfirst into the sea.

5 The Mystery Is Solved

I am a good swimmer. I did not lose my wits, either. First, I went straight down about twenty feet. Two strong strokes brought me to the surface, and I looked around. I could see the *Abraham Lincoln,* sailing away in the distance. I knew that I had not been noticed in the excitement. I was lost at sea, overboard.

Thinking this was the end of me, I began to yell for help. I kicked off my clothes so I could swim better.

All at once I realized that there was someone else in the water. I called and started to swim in that direction. It was Ned Land, of all people.

"There goes the frigate!" I yelled to him. "It's all over for us."

We swam around together. We wondered if anyone would miss us and have the frigate turned around to look for us. It was much to hope for, but still we hoped.

Suddenly an unbelievable thing happened. We found ourselves sitting on something that arose from the sea right under us. What a sensation that was!

"What is this we are sitting on?" I asked. "A floating island?"

"Professor, I think we are sitting on your narwhal," Ned said. "Here is my $2,000 prize. I'm sitting on it."

"Why, Ned," I yelled, "this beast is made of iron! Just feel it!"

My brain suddenly turned over. I kicked whatever we were sitting on. It was no animal. It didn't have scales, but it was covered with riveted plates made of iron. I could hardly believe my senses!

So it was not an animal at all, but an undersea ship. Men had made it, after all. This was the thing that had the whole world guessing. And here Ned and I were, sitting on it. We were the only ones who could solve the mystery of its origin and operation, and we were lost at sea!

If we had been sitting on an animal, I think we would not have been so surprised. But here we were, sitting on a man-made submarine which no one dreamed was in existence.

Suddenly the thing began to move, and to bubble. It was evidently run by a screw propeller at one end. We held on as well as we could, cruising along in the water.

"I hope it doesn't take a notion to dive!" I said.

"We'll be sunk if it does," Ned said. We both laughed at the joke, and it did us good to laugh.

"There must be people inside," said Ned. We could hear talking.

"There must be some way to let them know we are here," I said.

We felt around for an opening of some kind but could find none.

"I wonder what kind of people they are," said Ned.

"And I wonder what kind of engine this thing has," I said, "and how it goes."

The half-moon set as the night wore on. The submarine sailed straight ahead. Finally, when daylight came, we could see the hull. It had a platform.

Imagine our horror to feel the submarine sinking!

Ned Land swore loudly and yelled. We kicked the metal plates and stamped and yelled.

"Open up, you rascals! Open up this thing!"

When the water was about to our knees, the sinking stopped. The submarine rose to the surface. Then a grating noise came from inside. One iron plate moved aside, and a man appeared. He said something we could not understand. Then he disappeared.

Instantly he returned with eight strong men following him, wearing masks. They pulled us down inside the submarine. Quick as a wink it was over, and we were inside. I shivered. Who were these men? Were they pirates?

⑥ What Does "N" Stand For?

The panel closed behind us. We were in thick darkness: I could not see a thing. We went down a ladder. Where we were going, I could not even imagine. Feeling a floor beneath my feet, I groped about. We were in a closed room, in which there was no trace of a door or window.

Ned circled the room in the opposite direction, and we met. It was about twenty by ten feet. We bumped into a table and stools in the middle of it. We could not touch the ceiling.

Suddenly the lights came on. We looked up and saw an electric light in the ceiling. We heard the noise of bolts, and a concealed door opened. Two men entered. One later proved to be our captain, so I will describe him. He was the finest looking man I ever saw. I could not guess whether he was thirty-five or fifty, for he seemed to have no age. He was tall and deep-chested, with a fine build. He had good features too, with a particularly fine and beautiful set of teeth. His sharp, black eyes did not miss a thing around him.

The two men wore fur caps, sea boots, and woolen suits. They talked to each other in a language I could not understand. Then they began asking questions of us.

First I told our story in French, omitting nothing. I told who we were, where we had been, for how long, and why. I told about chasing the submarine. They lis-

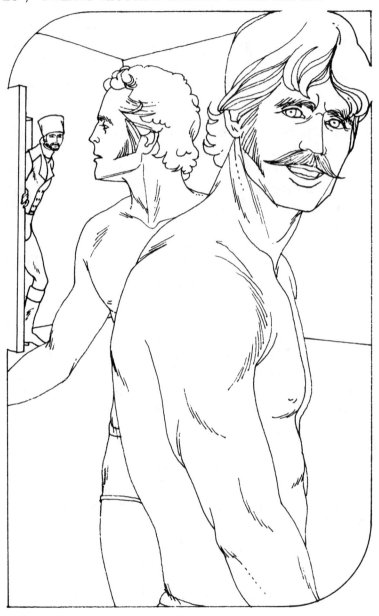

tened. However, they gave no sign of understanding a word we said.

Next, Ned told our story in English. Still there was not a sign of understanding. The third time, I told it in German, but still there was not one sign that the men knew what we said. I finished my story and looked at Ned.

"What will we do now?" he asked.

"Well, I'll try Latin this time," I said. "Many people study Latin in school. Maybe I can make them understand."

So I told the story for the fourth time, in Latin. The two strangers exchanged a few words in their unknown language. Then they left, shutting the door behind them.

"What luck!" said Ned. "We speak to those fellows in French, English, German, and Latin. But they don't know a word we said!"

"Well, I hope they understand that we are hungry. It is hours since we ate."

"What country do you think they are from? Could you tell?" asked Ned.

"I couldn't guess. They could be Spaniards, Turks, or Arabs. Their hair and skin are dark. But I never heard their language before."

A steward entered, bringing us coats and trousers, for we had stripped after we were thrown into the sea. While we were dressing, the steward set the table.

"What do you suppose these people eat—fish?"

"I don't care, for I'm nearly starved."

The meal was well served. It seemed like eating at a fine hotel in Paris. There was neither bread nor wine, however. We had fresh, clear water, and it tasted very good. Several dishes of delicious food were brought in. There were several kinds of fish, delicately cooked. Some of them I had never seen before. I could not tell what we were eating, but it tasted good. The table was beautifully set.

"Look at the silverware," said Ned. "Each spoon, fork, knife, and plate has the letter N engraved on it. I wonder what N stands for."

"It could be the first letter of the name of the submarine," I said, "or the initial of the commander of this sea bottom navy."

We were too hungry to talk much, but at least we knew the commander of the submarine was not going to let us starve. Afterward, we stretched out on a soft rug on the floor. Soon we were asleep. The last I remember was wondering if we were sinking to the bottom of the ocean. How strange it was to know that we were under the waves! Only a few feet away there were strange animals in the deepest beds of the sea. But I soon fell into a good sleep.

How long we slept I have no idea, but it seemed a very long time. I woke first and looked around. Ned had not moved. Nothing was changed. The air was so heavy that I was breathing with difficulty. We had evidently been asleep long enough to use most of the oxygen in the air.

How will the commander of this submarine renew our air supply? I wondered. Will he combine chemicals, or will we rise to the surface of the water, like a whale?

Even as I wondered, I felt fresh air in my lungs. I opened my mouth and gulped it. At the same time I felt the boat rolling. We had risen, just as I thought, to the surface for air. Well, I had figured out the ventilation system of the boat.

I saw the air pipe above the door. Volumes of fresh air poured in. It waked Ned who stretched and opened his eyes.

"What time do you think it is?" he asked.

"I have no idea. We slept a long time, maybe twenty-four hours. I'm hungry again."

It was about two hours before anyone came. We decided that the boat was propelled by an engine at one end. At any rate, we had felt the trembling of the hull when the propeller was in motion. Now the submarine lay quiet. We seemed to be plunged to the depths of the water. The silence was dreadful. We talked in whispers.

Suddenly we heard a grating noise, and two men came in. One was the steward. The other was the commander of the vessel. He spoke to us. And to our great surprise, he spoke in excellent French!

7   The Man of the Seas

"Professor Aronnax and Mr. Land," said the commander of the submarine, nodding to each one of us. "Will you be so good as to listen to me?"

You can imagine our surprise. We did not expect to hear our names called. We certainly did not expect to hear the French language, for we had thought no one understood us. Ned and I stood up. The commander leaned against a corner of the table, arms folded. He looked at us with his keen black eyes.

"Gentlemen," he said, "I speak English, French, German, and Latin. I could have talked to you in the first place. I understood every word you said. I wanted to hear your story, however, and take time to think it over."

This was surprising news. We listened sharply.

"I know who you are. You, sir, are Pierre Aronnax, professor of natural history. And you, sir, are Ned Land, a Canadian harpooner on board the frigate U.S.S. *Abraham Lincoln.*"

The man spoke easily and well, but I could tell that he was not a Frenchman.

"I have been thinking," he went on. "That is why I didn't come right back. I want you to know something about me too. I do not want you here. I did not ask you to come. I have broken all ties with human beings. You are a bother to me!"

30

"I can assure you," I spoke up, "that it was unintentional."

"Unintentional!" he said. "What do you mean? Was it unintentional that the U.S.S. *Abraham Lincoln* chased me all over the sea? Was it unintentional that you went on this trip? Was it unintentional that you shot at my vessel with a cannon? Was it unintentional that Ned Land struck me with a harpoon? It was your every intention to kill me!"

"Sir," I said, "you evidently don't know all the talk about you and your submarine in Europe and America. You evidently don't know how people wonder about you. Your submarine has destroyed many ships by ramming them. Maybe you don't know it, but we thought we were chasing a powerful sea monster. We thought we must rid the ocean of it, at any cost."

A half-smile curled his lips.

"Well, wouldn't you have destroyed a submarine as soon as a whale?"

I was embarrassed. I knew he was right.

"You understand, sir," continued the commander, "that I have a right to treat you as enemies?"

Again I answered nothing. What was there to say?

"This is why I have hesitated. I am under no obligation to you. I did not ask you to come here. I can put you back on the deck where I found you and sink once more into the sea. I can forget that you ever lived, and no one would know."

"That would be the deed of a savage," I answered him boldly. "You are civilized."

"Professor, I am not civilized. I have left civilization. I do not obey its laws. Don't ever mention civilization to me again."

I was amazed. I had a glimpse of a terrible past in the eyes of this man. He had put himself beyond all human laws, in the sea. Who would dare to pursue him? What ship could stand against his submarine? Who could bring him to trial? God (if he believed in God) and his conscience (if he had one) were his only laws. He was responsible to himself and God alone.

"I have thought for a long time," he finally said. "As human beings you are entitled to my pity. Since fate has

cast you here, you may remain. You did not ask to come here. But you will be free here in my submarine. In exchange for your liberty, there is only one condition. I will be satisfied with your word of honor."

"Well, sir," I asked, "what is your condition?"

"It may sometimes be necessary for you to stay in your cabins for hours or days at a time. I expect you to obey my orders. I take all the responsibility. But you cannot see certain things that will happen. Do you agree?"

Ah! Then things took place on this ship which we could not see! Well, that was not surprising.

"We accept," I said, "only I would like to ask one question."

"What is that?" he asked.

"You said we would be free on board your vessel."

"Entirely free," he said.

"But what do you mean by liberty, if we must be shut in our cabin sometimes?"

"You have the liberty to go, to come, to see everything with exceptions. You have the same liberty here that we enjoy."

"If you will pardon me," I said, "it seems that we are free to pace our floor in a prison. This is not enough."

"It must be enough, however," he said.

"What!" spoke up Ned. "Won't we ever see our country again, and our friends? What about our families and homes?"

"Oh, it is not so bad as you think, to give up your liberty," he said. "You are my prisoners of war. I could plunge you into the ocean, but I don't. You attacked me, remember. You came here to find out a secret which no man in the world must know. It is the secret of my whole life. Do you think I will let you go back when you know my secret? Never! I am keeping you!"

"I will be plain too, sir," I replied. "No word of honor binds us to you. We have only a choice between life and death—that is no choice at all. But you do not have our word of honor. We will escape if we can."

"You will have nothing to complain of here. You will find, Professor, among my favorite books, your own textbook on the depths of the sea," said the captain.

"What! You have my book! Do you like it?" I asked.

8   *More Surprises*

"Yes, I have often read it. You have carried your studies as far as anyone on land can do. But you do not know much about undersea life, Professor. You have seen only a small part of the depths of the sea. It is lucky for you that you are on my submarine. Now you will take a very long voyage. You can study undersea marvels."

This excited me, as I had not thought of it. He had touched my weak spot. True, I could learn a great deal on the voyage. It would make the loss of my liberty less important for a while.

"What are we to call you, sir?" I asked.

"I am Captain Nemo. My submarine is *The Nautilus*."

I remembered the letter *N* on the silverware and dishes. Captain Nemo called and a steward appeared. The Captain gave orders in the strange language they used.

"Our meal is waiting," he said to me. "We will follow this man."

Captain Nemo and I followed the steward to the dining room, where glassware and silver gleamed on white table linen. Captain Nemo pointed to a chair for me to sit on.

Most of the food on the table came from the sea, I

noticed, but I did not know what the dishes were, or how they were prepared. I tasted them and liked them.

"Sea food is good for you," said Captain Nemo. "For a long time now, I have eaten nothing but food from the sea. I am never sick any more. We are all healthy here, and we eat nothing but sea food."

"Does all your food come from the sea?" I asked.

"Yes, the sea provides all our needs. There are vast stores in the sea, which I have only to take. They are free. The Creator filled the sea with riches."

"Is this meat?" I asked. "It is delicious."

"It looks like beef, but it is turtle," he said. "Here are some dolphin livers that taste like pork. My cook is a clever fellow. And here is some excellent preserved seaweed. And this is cream from whale's milk. The sugar is from the great seaweeds of the North Sea, as good as any on land."

To be sure, I was pleased with the delicious, unusual meal.

"You like the sea, don't you, Captain?" I asked.

"I love it!" he exclaimed. "The sea is everything. It is eternal. It covers seven-tenths of the globe. It is a healthy place to live, and I am never lonely here. There is life everywhere in the sea—animals, vegetables, and minerals. It is Nature's vast reservoir, where all life began. Who knows but that life will end in the sea? Ah, the sea! In the sea there is great peace!" he said.

I listened with interest. Captain Nemo fascinated me.

"The sea does not belong to tyrants," he went on. "On the land men fight and tear each other to pieces. But thirty feet beneath the surface of the sea all men are equal. Their power is nothing. There is freedom in the sea—and equality. Ah, sir—if you would really live, live in the sea! Only in the sea is there freedom. Here there is no master! Here a man can be free!"

Captain Nemo was carried away by his love of the sea. Suddenly he became silent. He turned to me.

"Now, Professor," he said, "I will show you *The Nautilus.*" He rose.

I followed him into the next room, a beautiful library with a great many books.

"My books are at your service," he said. "I have works in every language."

"Thanks. I shall spend a great many hours here, reading."

"This is also a smoking room," he said. "Please accept this cigar."

"This is an excellent cigar," I said, as I lit it. "Is it from Havana?"

"No, this tobacco is made from a kind of seaweed I know of."

He opened another door, into a museum of undersea curios. In glass cases were dozens of specimens, some of which I had never seen before. I saw sponges shaped like vases and fans. They were wildly beautiful. I saw jellyfish and cases of beautiful corals. I saw starfish, sea cucumbers, and queer shells. Fine pictures hung on the walls, and I noticed a pipe organ also.

I remember a hammer shell, red and brown with white spots. It bristled with spines. It was very rare, worth several thousand dollars. I knew it from pictures.

In one case there were pearls—pink, green, yellow, blue, and black. Some were as large as a pigeon's egg and worth at least $600,000 apiece. I stared at them.

"Do you like my pearls?" asked Captain Nemo. "I have collected them myself. Every sea on earth has given me a pearl."

"No museum in Europe has such treasures as these," I said. "I do not wish to pry into your secrets, Captain, but I am deeply curious about *The Nautilus*. What makes it move? Will you tell me about the instruments that operate it? I see many things here that I would like to understand."

"I will be glad to tell you about them," he said. "But first, come and see your cabin. It is next to my own."

It was not really a cabin, but a fine room. It had a bed, dresser, and some other pieces of furniture. Ned's cabin was not far away.

Finally Captain Nemo took me to the navigation room, where the instruments which operated *The Nautilus* were. He pointed to a chair.

"Be so good as to sit down," he said. Then he began.

9 *All by Electricity*

"Sir," said Captain Nemo, "here are the instruments for navigating *The Nautilus*. I can instantly find my position and direction, in the middle of the ocean."

"Some of them I know already," I said. "This is a thermometer."

"Yes, it gives the temperature inside *The Nautilus*. The barometer forecasts changes in the weather, as you know. The hygrometer tells how much moisture is in the air."

"This compass guides your course," I said. "But what is this?"

"That is a sextant which tells our latitude by the sun. The chronometer here helps me figure longitude. With these powerful glasses I watch for ships."

"What is this?"

"A manometer to figure our depth. Everything here works by electricity. Light, heat, all the instruments—everything is electric."

"Electricity?" I cried in surprise. "That is amazing! What generates it?"

"Sea water. Chemicals in the sea produce electricity. It gives heat, light, motion, and even life itself to *The Nautilus*."

"But not air?" I asked.

"Oh, I could manufacture air by electricity," said the Captain. "But why do that? I go to the surface for air. This clock is electrical. It is better than any other kind. It is divided into twenty-four hours, but undersea there is no night or day. See, it is ten o'clock in the morning."

"Is this a speedometer?" I asked, pointing to a dial.

"Yes," he answered, "an electric connection with the propeller tells our speed. See! Now we are traveling at fifteen knots."

"It is marvelous, Captain," I said, "how electricity takes the place of wind, water, and steam for you."

"Now follow me to the stern, Professor," said the Captain.

He showed me how the rooms were separated by watertight walls. Each one could be shut off and sealed, in case of a leak.

"This ladder—what is it for?" I asked him.

"It leads to a good light boat. It is shut into a watertight compartment with a double opening. I get into the boat. Then I shut one door and open the other. My little boat shoots to the surface. Then I can fish or explore."

"How do you get back on board *The Nautilus*?" I asked.

"*The Nautilus* comes to me by orders. I telegraph to it."

Captain Nemo showed me a kitchen with an electric stove. Nearby there was a bathroom with hot and cold water.

"This electrical machine is a water distiller," said Captain Nemo. "It makes excellent drinking water. Would you like a drink?"

I drank a glass of the clear water he handed me. It was excellent. Next, he showed me the engine room. The generators were large and powerful. Electricity went forward to electromagnets of great size. One fly-wheel was nineteen feet across, with a thread twenty-three feet long. It could revolve 120 times per minute and was connected with the screw.

"*The Nautilus* can produce a terrific running speed," he explained.

"Yes, I remember. I saw *The Nautilus* play with the *Abraham Lincoln*. I knew your speed was greater than ours." He smiled.

"But how can you dive to great depths?" I asked. "And how do you stand the great pressures under the sea? And how do you get back to the surface?"

"Sit down here," he said. "I will show you the plan of *The Nautilus*. You see, it is a long cylinder with tapering ends. Its length is 230 feet, and its greatest width is 26 feet. Because it is long, narrow, and pointed, it glides easily in the water. It weighs fifteen hundred tons."

"Are the walls solid?" I asked. "And how thick are they?"

"There are really two walls. It is one submarine inside another, joined with T-shaped irons. It is stronger

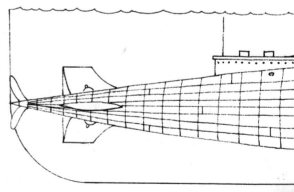

than if it were solid. It cannot cave in, either. The two hulls are made of steel two and a half inches thick. You see these chambers?" He pointed to the lower part of *The Nautilus.*

"These hold almost 166 tons of water. When they are full, the vessel sinks."

"But how do you let the water out again," I asked, "so you can rise?"

"It is hard to force this water out again, so we can rise. Electricity alone can give that power. The power of my electric engines is almost limitless. My pumps have enormous power. You saw the two jets of water shoot like a torrent, almost swamping the *Abraham Lincoln.* I have auxiliary reservoir chambers too. If I want to go down six or eight miles, I can."

"That is amazing!" I said. "How can you do that?"

"To steer this boat, I use an ordinary rudder behind the sternpost. I can also make *The Nautilus* rise and sink. I do this by two inclined planes on the sides, worked from the inside. If the planes are parallel, *The Nautilus* moves horizontally. If they are slanted, it sinks or rises diagonally. I can even go straight up."

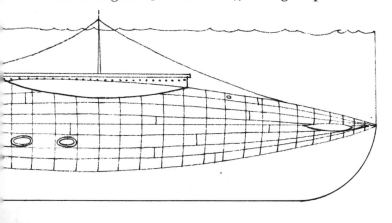

"But how can you see where you are going?"

"The helmsman is in a raised box, with lenses."

"Can they resist great pressure of the water?"

"Perfectly. Glass plates that are thin can resist unbelievably great pressures. But ours are over eight inches thick."

"But how can you see in the dark water?"

"We have a powerful reflector that throws light half a mile."

"Ah, and that explains the phosphorescence," I said. "Captain, *The Nautilus* is wonderful!"

"I am sorry about crippling the *Abraham Lincoln*. I hated to, but it attacked me. I could have sunk it, but I only put it out of commission. It can get to port for repair."

"You like *The Nautilus*, don't you?" I asked.

"Like *The Nautilus*! I love it! It is part of me! It is as firm as a rock. There are no sails to rip, no ropes and masts to break or blow away. There is no boiler to blow up. In the deep sea there are no storms. We cannot run short of fuel or water. Why, *The Nautilus* is perfect! I trust it because I built it myself. I am captain, builder, and engineer."

"But how could you have built it in secret?" I asked.

"Each separate part, Professor, was brought from a different part of the world. The keel was forged in France, the propeller in Scotland. The steel plates of the hull were made in Liverpool, and the tanks and reservoirs in France. The engine came from Germany, and the instruments from Sweden and New York. Each company had orders under different names."

"But all these parts had to be put together," I said.

"Professor, I set up my workshops on a desert island in the ocean. I taught my workmen myself. We put it together, and when we were through, we burned all traces."

"But the cost? It must have cost a great deal of money!"

"Yes, of course. It cost nearly a million dollars."

"One last question, Captain Nemo," I said. "Where did you get the money?"

"I am immensely rich," he replied. "I could pay the national debt of France without ever missing the money. Later, you will see—"

I stared at him. What an amazing person! Was he fooling me? Well, time would tell. At any rate, we were starting out on a long, long voyage together, for thousands of leagues under the sea.

10 *In the Japanese Current*

"Come on in, Ned, and sit down," I told him later that day. "I have many things to tell you." I began to repeat the amazing things the Captain had told me about *The Nautilus*.

"But tell me this, if you can," he said. "How many men are on board?"

"That I don't know. But if you are thinking of seizing *The Nautilus*, you'd better give up the idea. We are lucky to be here. Many people would like to be in our place. They would like to be on such a trip as this, to see the wonders we will see. We may as well make up our minds to make the best of it. We'll see—"

"See!" exclaimed the harpooner. "We'll see nothing. In this prison we might as well be blind, for all we can see! We haven't seen one thing yet but these walls."

At that instant, side panels slid open. There were two oblong openings with thick glass. Electric lights went on. The sea was clearly illuminated for miles.

What a spectacle! Who can describe what Ned and I saw? Who could describe the soft light, the transparent sea and its clearness? We looked out upon an immense aquarium, as clear as light itself. We could see for an almost endless distance.

"You wanted to see," I laughed. "Well, now you can."

For two hours we watched the undersea creatures. We marveled at their games, their beauty, their strangeness, their speed. I recognized a few of them, but only a few. I had never expected to see such creatures in their home in the sea. I cannot name or describe all we saw.

Attracted by the bright light, the fish swam to our window, their noses touching the glass. We stood amazed and watched and talked to them.

Then the panels closed again, and the vision disappeared. What wonders we had seen! For a long time we were unable to talk, after such marvels. Finally Ned spoke.

"Have you any idea where we are, Professor," he asked, "and where we are going? All I know is that we are in the Pacific Ocean."

"Yes, Ned. I'll show you. You know that seven-tenths of the globe is covered by the seas. You know that there are five great oceans: the Arctic and Antarctic, the Atlantic, the Pacific, and the Indian Ocean. Each ocean, you know, has its own current. Five great oceans, five great currents. They regulate the climate of the earth."

"Yes," said Ned impatiently, "and I know we are starting a long voyage that may last the rest of our lives. I don't know what difference it makes, but I'd like to know where we are."

"You know," I went on, "that the Pacific is the quietest of all the oceans. Its currents are broad and slow. It has medium tides and much rainfall."

"Yes, but where are we? I don't want a geography lesson."

"Here." I pointed to one of Captain Nemo's maps. "We're about two hundred miles from Japan now, in the Japanese Current. See, it starts here in the Gulf of Bengal, where the water is warmed by the tropical sun. It goes north along the coasts of Asia and turns into the Pacific Ocean, then to the Aleutian Islands."

Ned watched while I traced the warm Japanese Current with my finger. "Here is where it turns down the coast of North America. It gives the Pacific Coast a warm and pleasant climate."

"Then we are off to see the Japanese Current?" he asked.

"Yes," I answered. "It is this current that *The Nautilus* is to follow."

I was happy over the prospect, but I could see that Ned was not.

Dinner was soon served: turtle soup followed by several delicious sea food dishes. I ate them all with great enjoyment.

I passed the evening reading, writing, and thinking of the great wonders I had seen. I was determined to make the best of my imprisonment, to think of it as a chance to see the marvels of the deep sea. I was not going to waste time feeling sorry for myself.

Soon sleepy, I stretched out on the bed. I slept deeply. *The Nautilus* glided rapidly through the warm waters of the Japanese Current.

11 We Receive an Invitation

For the next few days I saw nothing of Captain Nemo. I spent my time studying in Captain Nemo's library. I began the records that make this book possible. But on the fifth day, I received a note from him. The writing was bold and clear. I opened it and read it.

November 16, 1867

To Professor Aronnax, on board
The Nautilus:

Captain Nemo invites Professor Aronnax to a hunting party, tomorrow morning, in the forests of Crespo Island. Mr Land is also invited.

Captain Nemo, Commander
The Nautilus

"A hunt!" said Ned, who was looking over my shoulder, "and on land! Well, once we are on dry ground, I know what I'll do—I'll escape! And I'll be glad to eat some real meat for a change. I'm tired of fish!"

"Let's see where Crespo Island is," I said, looking at the globe.

After some hunting we found it. It was a little dot lost in the North Pacific, about 1,800 miles from where we started.

"It may be dry ground, Ned, but Captain Nemo has chosen a desert island."

Ned shrugged his shoulders and left without a word. I knew he was discouraged.

When I woke up next morning, *The Nautilus* was still and the motors were shut off. I dressed and went to the dining room. Captain Nemo was there before me. He rose and bowed.

"Eat a hearty breakfast, Professor. There are no hotels on Crespo Island. We will not be back until very late this evening."

A hearty breakfast was laid, the usual sea food. But I was hungry and it tasted good.

"Today is our hunt in the submarine forests of Crespo Island," he began as I ate. "We have undersea suits, and an air supply to carry on our backs. There are two rubber tubes, one for fresh air and the other for foul air."

"How can we see our way?" I asked him.

"Fastened to your waist will be an electric storage battery. It gives a white and steady light. You will be able to breathe—you will be able to see."

"What gun will I carry for this hunt? How can I fire it?"

"An air gun with glass bullets is fired under great pressure. The pumps of *The Nautilus* furnish the pressure, of course. The glass bullets are deadly. Well, since you have finished, we will get into our undersea suits. We will soon be off."

12 We Walk on the Bottom of the Sea

Ned was not happy about going, I could see that. He saw two dreams fade away—the dream of escape, and the dream of eating fresh meat.

Two men came to help us put on the undersea suits. We could not have put them on by ourselves. They were two-piece suits made of heavy, seamless rubber to resist great pressure. Fastened to the trousers were thick boots with heavy soles of lead. There were gloves too, which were light enough not to be clumsy. There was, of course, a metal helmet with glass in front to see through.

I looked at the gun. It was a hollow steel tube with a valve worked by a spring that forced glass bullets into the barrel. When one bullet was fired, the next one went into position.

"Well, I am ready!" I said. "Show me the way to the bottom of the sea!"

"We have nothing to do but start," said Captain Nemo. "We are five fathoms deep."

With all my equipment, I was so heavy that I could not take one step. But I felt myself pushed into a little room, and a watertight door closed behind me. I heard a loud hiss, and we were shot out of the submarine through another door. In another instant our feet were outside, on the bottom of the sea.

Captain Nemo walked on ahead, with Ned and me following. We could not talk, of course, the entire day,

but made motions to each other. Once in the water my suit no longer felt heavy.

The sun shone through the water, making an unearthly colored glow. We could see well for more than a hundred yards in all directions. The water was clear and still.

Under our feet there was fine, even sand. It reflected the rays of the sun. We gradually lost sight of *The Nautilus,* and distant objects began to take form. Rocks, plants, and shells were everywhere—green, red, yellow, orange, purple, and blue. Some were prickly, some fell like drapes, some looked like lace, some like ribbons or flowers. Some even looked like jewels, they were so beautiful and sparkling. I hated to put my feet down, for I did not want to crush their beauty. I stopped to admire them, but Captain Nemo motioned for me to come on.

As we walked on, the ground was no longer sandy. Now it was ooze made of shells. Farther on again it would be a soft carpet made of seaweed. I remembered how many thousands of kinds of seaweed there are, but still I marveled to see so many. Green ones were near the surface, where they got the sun. Red ones were at a greater depth. In the deepest beds, the seaweed were brown or black.

By noon, when the rays of the sun were directly overhead, the magic colors changed. But now the earth sloped downward, and we were in water over a hundred yards deep. We could still see, but dimly. I had a feeling of mystery and wonder.

Captain Nemo stopped and waved his arm. He pointed to the dark shadows ahead.

"That must be the forest of Crespo Island," I thought.

And I was right.

13 We Hunt in the Submarine Forest

At last we were in the submarine forest which Captain Nemo called his own. Who could deny this? He was the first man to see it. No one could take it away from him. Besides his, few eyes ever saw it.

The forest, I found, was large seaweed the size of trees. All their branches grew straight up. They barely moved as they stretched to the surface.

I saw creatures I never had seen before. I could hardly tell plants from animals. Never had I seen such colors: pink, red, green, and brown. Some of the seaweed looked like ferns fifteen feet tall. Tiny fish played around in them.

For an hour we wandered about. Then Captain Nemo gave a signal to halt, and we stretched out to rest. We could not talk, of course. But I could see that Ned Land was enjoying himself. His eyes sparkled with delight, and he made comical faces to make me laugh. We lay down in the sand.

It is hard to believe, but we fell asleep. I was very tired, for our suits were heavy. I do not know how long we slept, but when we woke up the light had changed. It seemed to be nearly dark.

Suddenly, a few steps off, I saw a monstrous animal. It looked like a spider, only it was over three feet high. It was watching us, ready to spring. Captain Nemo waked just in time. He got to his knees. With the butt of his gun, he knocked the thing over. I saw it writhe in convulsions.

"I must be on my guard now," I thought. "There might be other monsters in these depths." I rose and followed Captain Nemo, who was walking on. The ground sloped down.

Suddenly we reached a deep, narrow valley, where the water was very clear. It was growing dark, and I was glad when a sudden, bright light came on. Captain Nemo had turned on his light, and Ned and I did the same. Then we walked on for three or four hours. Then we came to Crespo Island and stopped. Here was the end of Captain Nemo's domain, the sea. He refused to put his foot on land.

I saw Ned hesitate and look back as we turned. I knew he was thinking of escape. But it was useless to think of climbing that wall. We would only be on a desert island hundreds of miles from the path of ships. So we all started back to *The Nautilus*.

We went back by a different route. We saw one school of little fish that reminded me of birds. So far, we had seen nothing to shoot at. Suddenly I saw Captain Nemo raise his gun to his shoulder. Something moved into a bushy clump of seaweed. Then it suddenly fell, stunned. It was a fine sea otter, five feet long. It looked something like a beaver, only larger. I knew its fur was valuable, and I admired this strange animal with short ears and whiskers like a cat's.

Captain Nemo shouldered the beast, and we went on. Sometimes the water was so shallow that we could see clouds in the sky above. We could even see the shadows of birds flying low over the water in the evening sky.

By the sand underneath, I knew we were getting back to *The Nautilus*. All at once Captain Nemo turned and pushed me to the ground. Then he threw Ned, who had been walking beside me, to the ground also. I did not even have time to wonder what was the matter. Then I saw the captain lie down too, and remain motionless.

An enormous mass passed over us. It was phosphorescent. My blood froze. Two horrible sharks passed over us, as we lay too frightened to move. They were full

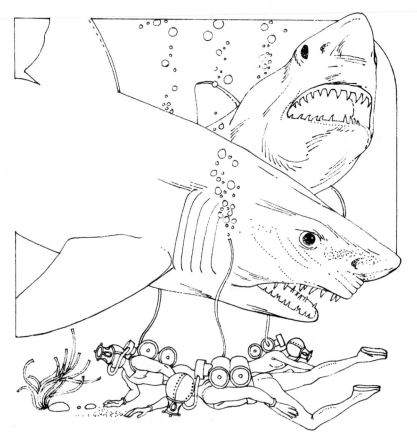

grown, with enormous jaws and dull, glassy eyes. Monstrous brutes—their iron jaws could crush a whole man! I could scarcely breathe. I noticed their huge mouths and cruel teeth, only inches away. Finally I saw their silver bellies pass over us, and then their enormous tails. We were possible victims, but they did not see us.

It is a good thing that this kind of shark does not see very well. I felt as if two tigers had passed by. When we rose again, my knees were weak from fright.

Half an hour later, we were back at *The Nautilus*. The outside door had been left open for us. We entered, and Captain Nemo closed the door. Then he pressed a knob, and I heard pumps working inside the submarine. Water sank rapidly around us.

In a few minutes the cell was drained. The inside door then opened, and we stepped inside.

The crew took our suits off us. Too tired to talk, I was quite hungry.

We fell to eating a delicious, hearty, hot meal. Each bite tasted better than the one before. At last I was full of good food, and full of wonder. What a day we had spent! I could hardly believe what my own eyes had seen.

Though it was still early, I went straight to bed and fell asleep immediately.

14 Four Thousand Leagues Under the Sea

For days and weeks after our hunting expedition I hardly saw Captain Nemo. I could follow our course on the chart, so I always knew where we were. The side panels were opened every day. Ned and I never tired of watching the mysterious creatures of the undersea world. I took many notes, of course, for my book.

Our general direction was southeast. By and by we saw the largest of the Hawaiian Islands at a distance. I saw the volcanoes and mountain ranges of those beautiful islands, which rise fifteen hundred feet above the sea. We did not go close, however.

Still we continued southeast. Finally we saw the Marquesas Islands in the South Pacific. One night Ned called to me, as he stood looking out the panel under the sea.

"Look there! A ship! A shipwreck!"

To be sure, there was a shipwreck before our very eyes. It hung in the water, with its tattered sails still hanging from the chains. The three masts had broken off. It was a sad sight. Saddest of all were the corpses on the bridge. I counted six—four men and a woman with a baby in her arms. The poor little thing still had its arms around her neck. The men were sailors, and one was at the helm. They were tied with ropes to the vessel. Their story was plain to Ned, who had been through terrible storms at sea.

"It must have been a terrible storm they were in," he said. "They tied themselves to the masts, to keep from being washed overboard. It was just recently, too, for the barnacles haven't even started to cover the wreck."

"The helmsman!" I said. "He seems to be steering the ship straight to the bottom of the sea."

What a scene! We shuddered. Even as we looked, we could see hungry sharks coming, with hungry eyes and ugly mouths. They were attracted by the human flesh.

This was only the first one of many wrecks that we saw on our voyage with Captain Nemo. It was always a horrible spectacle to see the hull of a ship rotting in the depths, eaten up by rust and covered with barnacles.

Finally we were in the coral islands of the South Pacific. Ned and I were looking at the corals one day as I was explaining how the little coral animals build land. The daily work of these tiny sea animals is to make a bit of rock. Their bit is joined to the bit made by millions of others. A coral reef is slowly built in this way. Then this new island will be joined to other groups nearby. Some day a new continent will stretch into these waters.

"How long does it take these huge coral reefs to be built?" asked Ned.

"About one-eighth of an inch in a hundred years," I told him.

"Why, that's only one inch in eight hundred years!" he exclaimed.

"Is that hard to believe?" I asked. "Nature isn't in a hurry."

Just then Captain Nemo came by. He heard us discussing the corals.

"The earth does not want new continents," he said coldly. "It wants new men!"

Ned and I often wondered what terrible tragedy had made the Captain so unhappy.

On and on we went. Finally we turned to the west. We saw beautiful Tahiti, graceful island, queen of the Pacific. We did not go near, but I saw the high mountains on the island. Fish were plentiful here, and delicious too.

Christmas came and went without notice.

15 We Run Aground

Early on the morning of January 1, Ned met me on the platform.

"Happy New Year, Ned!" I said to him.

"What do you mean—happy—under the circumstances?" he asked. "Do you mean an end to our prison life, or some more sightseeing?"

"I hardly know how to answer," I told him. "We are sure to see many more sights. Each one is more wonderful than the last, to me. I don't know when our trip will end."

"Well, a happy new year for me would be to get out of this prison," he said.

We had now come 11,340 miles, or 5,250 leagues, since our voyage started in the Japanese Current. Before us stretched the dangerous coral reefs off the northeast coast of Australia. The Barrier Reef is 360 miles long. The sea breaks against it like thunder, and the water is always rough and dangerous. Ships never venture into these rough seas, but there are many interesting animals and plants. I never tired of looking at them as we cruised along.

Captain Nemo had told me that he was going to the Indian Ocean by crossing through Torres Strait. The Strait is nearly thirty-five leagues wide, and navigation is very hard. Many islands, reefs, and rocks, besides the rough water, make it dangerous.

Ned and I went up one day to the platform, taking

the big map with us. *The Nautilus* was cruising slowly. Captain Nemo was there, looking thoughtful.

"This is a bad sea!" remarked Ned. "This coral could pierce our sides."

The situation indeed looked dangerous. Captain Nemo was directing our course, and *The Nautilus* slid like magic between the rocks. Suddenly there was a bump, which threw me off my feet. *The Nautilus* had touched upon a coral reef. Captain Nemo and some of the crew were looking over the side, talking in their queer language. Ned and I could never learn it, but Ned called it submarine language.

We looked too. We had run aground. It looked like a sorry situation to me: *The Nautilus* had not been damaged, but she could not get off the rock.

"An accident, Captain?" I asked.

"Hardly an accident," he replied. "Just an incident, nothing serious."

"But we are aground in the open sea," I said. "The tides are not strong in the Pacific. I do not see how you can get off."

"You are right, Professor," he answered, "the tides are not strong in the Pacific. But here in Torres Strait there is a difference of a yard and a half between high and low tide. In five days the moon will be full. The moon will raise the tide enough to get us off."

Captain Nemo left, followed by his lieutenant.

"Well, Ned, now we will wait patiently for the tide in five days. Then the full moon will pull us off again. I hope you're not in a hurry!"

"Really?" he asked, for we were both impatient. "You can believe me, Pierre. This piece of steel will never navigate again, under the sea or on the sea. It is fit for junk only. I think that the time has come for you and me to part company with the captain. Are you agreed?"

"Well, Ned, I don't know whether the moon can pull us off. But I know one thing. If we were in sight of the coast of France, we might do well to escape now. But look where we are! We are in Australian waters. Ships never come here. No one would ever pick us up. First, let's see if the moon pulls us off the reef. Then if it doesn't, we'll talk about escape."

Ned agreed that there was nothing else for us to do but wait and see.

"I'll tell you what let's do," he said. "Over on that

island there are trees. And under the trees there might be land animals. Some of the land animals might be pigs. And pigs would mean pork chops, or roasts. Why don't you ask Captain Nemo's permission for us to go hunting over there on land?"

It sounded like a good idea, and to our surprise the captain was very pleasant about it. He said we could go. Of course, he knew that we would not be foolish enough to escape across New Guinea. We were better off as prisoners on *The Nautilus* than in the stewpot of South Sea cannibals.

So we left *The Nautilus*, rowing in a dinghy. The sea was calm, and Ned was happy. You would almost have thought he was escaping.

"Ah, meat!" he cried. "We are going to eat some real meat!"

"Ned," I laughed, "I believe your teeth are sharpened like a hatchet. All you think of is meat. We have had good food—don't you like fish?"

"Fish is all right—once in a while," he said. "But a piece of fresh venison grilled on the live coals—oh, I can taste it now!"

"We shall see," I told him. "Maybe those forests are full of game. But maybe the game will hunt us. Maybe there are tigers!"

"Tigers? Why, I will eat tigers too. I like tiger meat. Fresh loin of tiger! Ah, I will shoot the tiger, cook it, and eat it!" he said, smacking his lips.

In half an hour, our little dinghy ran up on the sand. We had passed the coral reef and we alighted on the beach of Gueboroar Island.

16 A Few Days on Land

After two months as prisoners on *The Nautilus*, it was good to be on land again. Ned stooped over and rubbed his hands in the sand. He filled his fists with it and threw it. We looked all around us.

Back from the beach, we could see enormous trees tied together with vines. Palms, ferns, and orchids were everywhere. Ned found a coconut and broke it open. We drank the milk and ate the meat. It was good. We saw no sign of people.

"Look at what I found!" yelled Ned. "Breadfruit!"

In each hand he held a breadfruit, each one over a foot long and six inches thick. They reminded me of small melons.

"What luck! Now we can eat, if we can make a fire. I always wanted to taste breadfruit."

"This is the best kind," Ned said, cutting one open. "See, it has no seeds. It tastes the best too—I've eaten it before. I know how to cook it. I'll make a fire." He was busy with some sticks.

While the fire was burning down to coals, we brought in some fine, ripe breadfruit. We sliced it and laid it on the red coals.

"You will see how good this is," said Ned. "It tastes better than cake. If you don't come back for more, I'm no longer king of harpooners."

Ned was right. In a few minutes the breadfruit was

67

roasted. We ate it all with great relish. Its soft, white crumbs reminded me of fresh cake.

"It must be long past noon," I said, looking at the sun. "Why don't we take some of these back to the submarine?"

Ned thought that was a good idea. So we gathered a pile of breadfruit to carry to the boat. Then we raided the cabbage palms. In the green tip of each is a delicious, tender heart. When this is cooked, it tastes like cabbage. We also found some wild yams that looked like sweet potatoes. We took several coconuts too.

Toward evening, we started carrying our food over to *The Nautilus* in the boat. We could see no one around. The submarine seemed deserted. We loaded our food on the deck; then went to our cabins to sleep.

The next day there was still no sign of life on *The Nautilus,* so Ned and I decided to go back to the island. This time we took a different direction to explore. We came to a thick wood where parrots were, chattering together and flying from branch to branch.

"Look over there, Ned." I pointed.

A young parrot, bright green in color, sat on a branch. He was talking to a red and white cockatoo. The cockatoo listened wisely to him, cocking his head as if thinking. He looked at the parrot out of the corner of his eye.

"The old cockatoo doesn't believe a word the parrot is saying," Ned said. "But he is too polite to say so."

We passed through some bushes and came to a little clearing. Here we saw birds of paradise as large as peacocks, and as beautiful. They had graceful curves and fine colors—yellow beak, purple-tipped wings, yellow and green neck. No wonder the natives value them so highly.

The only game we saw were some pigeons. Ned shot two. They had been eating nutmeg, which he said would give them a good flavor.

Ned was still hunting for red meat. Finally he

found it. About two o'clock he shot a fine big hog. Delighted, he cleaned it and skinned it. Then he cut six cutlets. Ned understood all about cooking outdoors; to add to our feast, he brought in some kangaroos which he found in the bushes. He roasted all our food over the fire while I was busy carrying wood and helping him. We had pigeons, breadfruit, cabbage palm, coconut milk and meat, pork cutlets, and kangaroo. What a feast!

We finished off our meal with some wild pineapples I had found. We ate our fill and stretched out on the sand.

"Suppose we stay here on the island tonight?" I said.

"Suppose we don't go back at all?" he said. "Suppose we just stay here?"

Just then a stone fell between us.

17 *Captain Nemo's Thunderbolt*

Stones do not fall from the sky. Then a second stone fell. We jumped up.

Savages! About twenty of them came running through the bushes about twenty yards away. They were armed with bows and slings.

In less than two minutes we were on the shore where our dinghy was moored. Ned grabbed the roast pig and we ran. The natives chased us, running and yelling. Now there were 100 or more.

In an instant we pushed the boat out to sea, jumped in, and began rowing as hard as we could. The natives, howling, followed up to their waists into the water.

I looked at *The Nautilus*, to see if our noise had attracted anyone there. But no one appeared. We were soon on board, pulling our boat in after us. Hearing music, I went down to the drawing room. Captain Nemo was there, playing his organ.

"Captain!" I said, touching his hand.

"Ah, it is you! Have you had a good hunt?" he asked calmly.

"Yes, but unfortunately we disturbed some savages. They chased us on board."

"Savages? Don't be surprised at finding savages. There are savages everywhere. But these are less harmful than the savages we left behind in your country."

"But Captain!" I said. "There are at least 100 of them, and they are armed!"

"*The Nautilus* has nothing to fear," he said, and went right on playing.

I did not understand him. He did not seem excited, but here we were grounded on a coral reef, surrounded by howling savages on the shore nearby.

Next morning I went up on the platform early. I saw the natives still on the shore. Some of them had come very near the submarine, to the coral rock where we were grounded. They were of good build, with large, high foreheads. Their wooly hair had a reddish tinge, and bones hung from their ears. Their bodies were naked. Some had collars of red and white glass beads. All were armed with bows and arrows, or shields. They carried around their necks bags full of stones to use in slings.

They motioned for me to come on land, but I shook my head. About noon the tide rose. They went back to the shore. By this time, there were 500 or 600 of them. They evidently did not know what to think of *The Nautilus*. They had probably seen European ships before, but not a submarine. Finally a score of canoes surrounded us. They were scooped out of tree trunks, and were fast and well-balanced. Half-naked natives paddled them. A shower of arrows fell on us.

I went down to the captain's room and knocked at the door.

"Come in," said Captain Nemo.

I entered. He had some papers spread out before him. He was figuring in algebra. I recognized x and other signs.

"I'm sorry to disturb you, Captain," I said, "but the

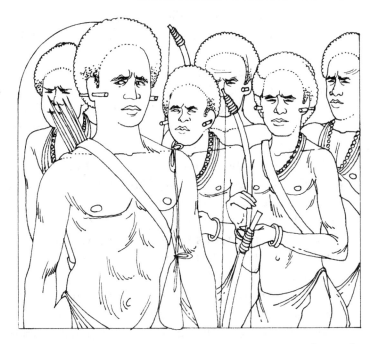

natives are surrounding us in their canoes. In a few minutes they are going to attack."

"Well, then we must close the hatches. But do not worry, Professor. These gentlemen will not hurt *The Nautilus.*"

He pressed an electric button and gave orders to one of the crew.

"But Captain, tomorrow we must open the hatches to get fresh air. What is to prevent the natives from entering through the hatches?"

"Tomorrow, at twenty minutes before 3 P.M., *The Nautilus* will float. Then we will leave the Straits of Torres unharmed. I do not want one of these natives hurt."

He rose and left. I went to find Ned, as I wanted to

tell him. He was in the galley, cooking some of the breadfruit we had brought on board. I told him what Captain Nemo had said.

"Do you believe that *The Nautilus* will float free of this coral reef tomorrow?"

"I don't know, Ned," I said. "All we can do is hope the captain is right. We have to trust him now, and try to sleep tonight with all this noise."

All night long the natives stamped on the platform. They howled and beat on *The Nautilus* until I could hardly sleep. But no one else seemed to worry.

At six I rose. The hatches had not been opened, but when the emergency tanks were released, we got several cubic feet of fresh air. I stayed in my room until noon. I was very restless, but finally 2:30 P.M. came. If Captain Nemo was right, we would be off the coral reef in ten minutes. If not—well, our situation looked bad.

Soon *The Nautilus* began to vibrate. Then I heard the keel grate against the reef. Captain Nemo appeared at my door.

"We are starting now," he said. "I gave orders to open the hatches."

"How about the natives? Won't they come inside?"

"Come and see, Professor. Then you will understand."

I went with him. The crew was opening the hatches. The natives were howling. One native put his hand on the railing. Then, as if struck, he turned and fled, screaming. Ten more natives tried to enter. They met the same fate. Ned was excited. He too rushed to the staircase and seized the railing. He too was knocked over.

"I am struck with a thunderbolt!" he yelled.

Now I understood. It was not a thunderbolt at all. The rail was charged with electricity. Whoever touched it received a severe shock.

"Now you see?" asked Captain Nemo. "Electricity made a barrier to protect me. It would not kill anyone, but no one could pass through it without a severe shock."

The natives retreated in fear, and we were relieved. Ned rubbed his hand.

"That was the shock of my life," he said. He could always make a joke.

At this moment *The Nautilus*, raised by the high tide, left the coral reef. It was twenty minutes before 3 P.M., exactly. No ship could have left her mooring more on schedule.

She went slowly at first, then increased speed rapidly. Thus we left the dangerous waters of the Torres Strait safe and sound.

18   *We Are Locked Up*

The Nautilus was indeed a wonderful vessel. Electricity not only ran it, heated it, lighted it, aired it, but also protected it from attack. I was full of admiration for the submarine. I admired Captain Nemo, too, for he had thought of it, built it, and operated it.

Now we were going west, the Torres Strait behind us. We were near the Gulf of Carpentaria, on the north coast of Australia. There were still many reefs. On January 13, we saw the Island of Timor. Then we turned southwest to the Indian Ocean. Where were we going? Would we return to Asia? Would we go to Europe? Would we go south to the Antarctic? Time alone would tell, for Captain Nemo told us nothing.

The days passed quickly. Like snails, we were fastened to our shell, *The Nautilus*. We thought no longer of life on land, only of our daily life on the submarine.

On January 18, a strange thing happened. The barometer had been going down for days, so we knew a storm was coming. The weather was bad and getting worse. I went up to the platform. Captain Nemo was looking through his glass toward the horizon. He and the lieutenant were talking. Captain Nemo was cool, but the lieutenant was excited. They pointed, but I could see nothing on the horizon. We were hundreds of miles from land, so I wondered what they could see through their glasses.

Captain Nemo gave an order, and *The Nautilus* increased its speed. I went below and brought up another pair of glasses to look through. When Captain Nemo saw the glasses, he snatched them away from me. I turned toward him in surprise. I hardly recognized him, for his eyes were blazing with anger. His teeth were set. I could tell that he was greatly aroused. Had I discovered some secret?

"Professor," he said crossly, "you and your companion must be shut up in your room until I release you."

"Yes, sir," I replied. "But may I ask one question?"

"None, sir," he said.

Ned and I went down to my cabin. The door was shut on us and locked from the outside. We were astonished. We could not explain what we had seen.

We ate supper in silence. I felt a strange fear. What was happening?

Just then the lights went out, and we were in utter darkness. I felt my way to my bed. Suddenly I had become very sleepy. A painful suspicion seized me. I had been drugged! Imprisonment was not enough—Captain Nemo had drugged me to sleep.

I called to Ned, but he was already asleep. I tried to stay awake, but it was impossible. My breathing grew weak. My limbs became numb and cold. My eyes felt like lead. Then I fell into unconsciousness.

19 *The Coral Cemetery*

The next day I woke. My head felt clear, but I remembered nothing whatever that had happened. Wondering if I was still a prisoner, I tried the door. It opened. I was quite free, so I went up to the platform. Ned was there ahead of me.

Like me, Ned remembered nothing. *The Nautilus* seemed quiet. There was a mysterious quietness, but we noticed no change.

About two that afternoon, Captain Nemo came to my door. He looked tired and very sad. Restless and uneasy, he paced the floor before he spoke.

"Are you a doctor, Professor?" he asked me.

"Well, in a way. I practiced medicine for a few years." I stared at him.

"Will you kindly look at one of my men?" he asked. "He is ill."

I followed him with my heart pounding. I knew there must be some connection between the illness of one of the crew and what had happened the day before.

Captain Nemo took me to a cabin near the sailors' quarters. There lay a man about forty years of age. He was wounded. His head was bandaged and bloody with a horrible injury. His skull was shattered, and the brain was exposed. Great clots of blood were in the wound. The man's breathing was slow and painful. I felt his pulse, but it was weak and uneven. His legs felt cold. I knew that he was near death. I put a blanket over him. He was unconscious, of course.

"What caused this wound?" I asked the captain.

"What difference does that make?" asked Captain Nemo.

"Nothing can save him. He will be dead in two hours."

"There was a—a shock, a collision. One of the gears was broken. It struck this man," said Captain Nemo.

Tears came to the captain's eyes, and he clenched his fist. I did not suppose that he could shed tears.

The man grew more pale as his life slowly ebbed away. I sat by his side. His face was intelligent, but it was deeply troubled. He muttered some words, but I could not understand them. What was the secret of this man's life? What was the secret of his death? By and by, he ceased breathing, and I covered his face.

"You can go now, Professor," said the captain.

I returned to my room, deeply shocked by what I had seen. All day long I had terrible thoughts. All that night I had horrible dreams.

Next morning Captain Nemo was waiting for me on the deck.

"Professor, will you make an undersea trip today? Ned Land may come too, if he likes."

"We obey your orders, Captain."

"Then be so good as to put on your cork jackets."

In half an hour we were ready. Captain Nemo and a dozen of the crew were ready also. We set out on foot, as before, about thirty feet under the sea. The Nautilus was resting on the bottom of the ocean.

The bottom here was coral reef, and the light made

a thousand brilliant colors. Truly it was a garden in bloom, only in coral. Fish swam all about us. I reached out my hand to pick some of the gorgeous and delicate sea flowers. When my hand drew near, however, they closed up. By chance, I was seeing the most precious and beautiful corals in the world. I wondered where we were going.

We walked about two hours. Our depth was about 300 yards in an immense forest of corals and huge seaweed. What a sight!

Finally Captain Nemo stopped, and his men formed a circle around him. Then I noticed that they carried a large oblong object on their shoulders. Captain Nemo gave a signal to one of the men, who stepped forward and began to dig with a pickax.

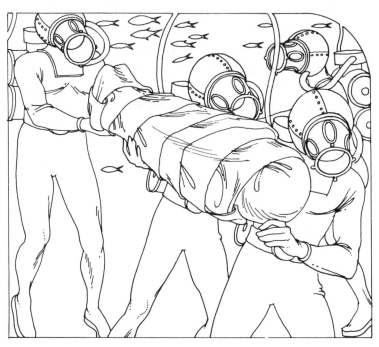

This was a cemetery! The man was digging a tomb! The oblong object was the body of the man I had seen die of his wounds! The captain and his men had come to bury their comrade. Here would be his grave, at the bottom of an unknown ocean.

Finally the tomb was dug. Then the bearers approached. The body, wrapped in canvas, was lowered into the coral grave. The captain and the others knelt in prayer.

Then the grave was filled. Again the men knelt in a last farewell. Then the funeral procession returned to *The Nautilus.*

When we had returned, I changed my clothes and went up to the platform. Captain Nemo was there, staring at the water sadly.

"That was the man I saw last night?" I asked.

"Yes, Professor. He rests now near his companions in our coral cemetery. He is forgotten, but not by his friends here. The corals will seal his grave forever."

He buried his face in his hands.

"Your dead sleep quietly, Captain, out of the reach of sharks."

"Yes, Professor. Out of reach of sharks—and men!" he replied.

Part 2

1 In the Indian Ocean

Now we come to the second part of our journey under the sea in *The Nautilus*. The first part ended in the coral cemetery. The funeral made a deep impression on me. In the sea, united in death as in life, the crew left their friend.

"What do you think about Captain Nemo now?" I asked Ned.

"Sometimes I think he hates the world because it has not noticed him. Maybe he is a genius that people don't understand. Maybe he is tired of the world and took to the sea, where he can do as he pleases. What do you think?"

"It looks to me as if there is more to it than that," I replied. "He shuns people—that is true. But he is also trying to get even with the world. Why?"

"It is clear to me that we were drugged and shut into our rooms that night. The captain wanted us out of the way for something."

"Yes, I agree. And his snatching the glasses out of my hand indicates that he didn't want me to see whatever was on the horizon. What it was, I can't imagine. And the man who was wounded—you know, I think that was the result of some mysterious shock on *The Nautilus*."

"Do you think we rammed a ship?" asked Ned.

"Who knows? Nothing is clear to me."

At that time, our course was west in the Indian Ocean. On we went for many days. Loving the sea, I took daily walks on the platform to get fresh air and see the bright waters. Cutting the equator at the eighty-second meridian, we entered the Northern Hemisphere. One day a horrible troop of sharks followed us. They were brown with grey bellies, some eighteen or twenty feet long. But *The Nautilus* increased its speed and left them behind.

Late in February we were near the island of Ceylon.

"The island of Ceylon is noted for pearl fisheries, Professor," remarked Captain Nemo, who was leaning over the map. "Would you care to visit a pearl fishery?"

Both Ned and I were eager to go.

"By the way, are you afraid of sharks?" asked the captain of Ned.

"Sharks!"

"Pearl hunting is full of thrills," said the captain, "and sharks are one of them. But we will be armed." Ned looked at me sourly behind the captain's back.

"Professor, what makes some oysters contain pearls?" Ned asked me later.

"There is a grain of sand in the flesh of the oyster," I told him. "It hurts the oyster, which deposits the pearly matter, year after year, in thin layers around the grain of sand."

"Can an oyster have more than one pearl?"

"Oh, yes. A single oyster can have a hundred and fifty pearls," I told him. "They vary in price according to size, color, and polish."

2   *A Pearl of Great Price*

Early next morning we left for our pearl-fishing trip—Captain Nemo, five sailors, Ned, and I. For some distance we went in the dinghy, arriving soon at our destination.

"Now we will put on our diving suits and begin our walk," said Captain Nemo. "We will not need lights, for we will be in shallow water. We won't take guns, but here is a strong knife to put in your belt. Now we start!"

We followed as Captain Nemo led us into the waves. In an hour or so we came to the oyster beds. Here pearl oysters are cultivated by the millions.

We came to a large cave in the rocks. Captain Nemo entered first, and we followed him. In the bottom of a pit, within the cave, we saw an oyster of about 750 pounds. The shell was seven feet wide. The oyster it contained must have weighed 35 pounds.

Captain Nemo evidently knew about this oyster. He seemed to have been here many times before. He put his dagger between the shells, then he opened them. I saw a pearl as large as a coconut. It was clear and beautiful, a gem of great worth. I stretched out my hand, just to touch the beautiful pearl. But Captain Nemo shook his head. The oyster closed again as he drew back his dagger. I understood. He was leaving the pearl to grow some more. Each year it would increase in size and weight. I estimated its value as two million dollars.

Outside the cave, I saw something surprising. An Indian fisherman came by in his canoe. He dived, holding a stone between his feet. A rope fastened him to the boat. When he reached the bottom (about five yards from the surface) he filled his bag with oysters. Then, pulling the stone after him, he rose to the surface, back to his boat. He did not see us hiding behind the rocks. Wouldn't he have been surprised to know that we were watching him? He knew of no one else about.

Suddenly I saw him rise in terror. He made a spring to return to the surface of the sea, to his boat. A gigantic shadow appeared over him: a shark of enormous size. Stiff with horror, I was unable to move.

The hungry shark shot toward the Indian diver. Striking him on the chest with its tail, the shark turned around, turned over on its back, and prepared to bite the man in two.

Suddenly Captain Nemo rose. Dagger in hand, he went straight for the monster, face to face. Seeing his new enemy, the shark turned over again. It made straight for Captain Nemo.

I can still see Captain Nemo, waiting there for the shark. When it rushed at him, he threw himself to one side, and it swam on past. Then he buried his dagger deep into its side. A terrible combat followed.

The shark seemed to roar. Blood rushed in torrents from its wound, until the sea was red. Then the captain held on to one of the shark's fins, dealing one blow after another to his enemy.

The shark struggled wildly. I was nailed to the spot with horror.

Once the shark upset him, and he fell to the sea floor. The shark's jaws opened wide, like a pair of factory shears.

It would soon have been over for Captain Nemo. But quick as a wink, Ned Land rushed toward the shark and struck it with his harpoon, which he had brought along.

Then the waves were flooded with the shark's blood. Ned's aim was true—as it always was. The shark was dead.

Captain Nemo rose to his feet without a wound. He went straight to the Indian pearl fisher. Cutting the cord that held the poor man to his stone, the captain took the native in his arms. With a quick jump he rose to the surface, and we followed.

We brought the unfortunate man back to life. Imagine his horror, when he opened his eyes, to see the copper helmets of our diving suits bending over him. What do you suppose he thought? He must have thought he had awakened in another world of strange men.

Captain Nemo drew from his pocket a bag of pearls. This he placed in the Indian fisherman's hand, where he would find it when he felt stronger. Then we returned to the water. In an hour we were back at *The Nautilus*, taking off our suits.

"Thank you, Mr. Land," said Captain Nemo.

"It was in return for my own life, remember," said Ned. "I owed you that."

From the platform we could see the shark's body floating on the surface. It was more than twenty-five feet long, with an enormous mouth. A dozen more sharks came, as we watched. Throwing themselves upon the dead shark, they tore it to pieces.

"Captain Nemo," I said, "I admire your courage. Never have I seen such courage in my life. You risked your own life to save an unknown human being, a poor man."

"Professor," he answered, "it is true that I have fled from the world of men. It is true that I hate civilization. Still, I pitied this poor Indian fisherman. He comes from an oppressed country. I am, and always will be, one of the oppressed."

3 We Cross the Red Sea

We left the island of Ceylon on January 29. Since we started on *The Nautilus*, we had come 16,220 miles, or 7,500 leagues. How many more we had to go, we had no way of knowing. For all we knew, we were prisoners for life.

Traveling north by northwest toward the Gulf of Oman, between Arabia and India, we came to the surface. No land was in sight.

"Where are we going now?" Ned wanted to know. "The Persian Gulf has no outlet. We will just have to turn around and go back."

"I have no idea. Captain Nemo has not said. We go where he takes a fancy."

"I need not tell you, Pierre, the Red Sea is closed too. The Suez Canal has not been cut yet. It is just being talked about. Even if it were cut, Captain Nemo would not use it—you know that."

"Maybe we will just turn around again. Maybe we will go back to the Indian Ocean. Maybe we will go down the coast of Africa, to the Cape of Good Hope."

"And after the Cape of Good Hope—what then?" he asked.

"Into the Atlantic Ocean, I suppose," I said. "Ned, I know that you are tired of our journey under the sea in *The Nautilus*. You have had enough submarine wonders."

"Well, aren't you tired of it too? Wouldn't you like to go home?" he asked.

"To tell the truth, Ned, I shall be sorry to see our voyage come to an end. Few men ever had such an opportunity as we have had."

For four days we cruised around in the Gulf of Oman, at different depths and speeds. We saw cities, but always several miles from land.

Finally we entered the Red Sea and saw the city of Mokha. Then we approached the shore of Africa. I passed many hours at the submarine window, for the

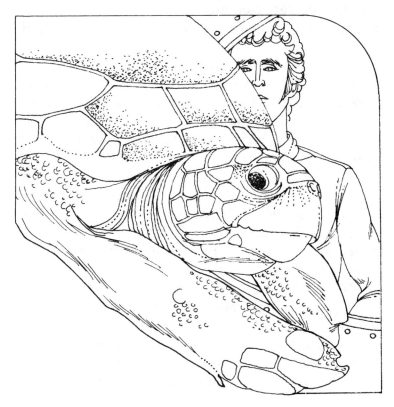

undersea plants and animals in these waters are beautiful to behold.

There were sponges of all shapes. Fishermen give them beautiful names, such as basket, elk horn, lion's feet, peacock's tail. Some were like a man's hand. Some were like leaves of a tree. Fish and turtles brought on board made delicious food.

"Well, Professor, does the Red Sea please you? Have you seen enough of its wonders? Do you like its sponges, corals, and fish?" the captain asked one day.

"Yes, Captain Nemo," I answered. "*The Nautilus* is a wonderful ship. Nothing can hurt it—neither storms, coral rocks, people, nor ordinary ships. It is a great invention."

"There is nothing else like it in the world," said Captain Nemo. "But who knows if, in another hundred years, the world will not see another *Nautilus*? Progress is slow, Professor Aronnax."

"It is true," I answered, "your submarine is at least a hundred years ahead of its time. The first men sailed the sea on a raft. They had no instruments for navigation. They did not know the sea, so they feared it. By the way, where did the Red Sea get its name?"

"From the microscopic plants that live in it," he answered. "There are a million in one square inch. I have seen the sea as red as blood."

"Have you been in the Red Sea before?" I asked.

"Oh, yes, many times."

"Tell me, have you ever seen any signs under the water of the Egyptian army that was swallowed up by the Red Sea? They chased the Israelites, according to the Bible story. Moses commanded the waters of the Red

Sea to part. The Israelites crossed on the sand. But when the Egyptians followed, they were swallowed up. Tell me, have you seen any signs of the army of Pharaoh?"

"No, Professor, I have not. The water there is too shallow. But maybe if you dug in the sand, at the Isthmus of Suez, you would find arms and utensils of the Egyptians."

"Before long the Suez Canal will be dug at that point," I said.

"Unfortunately, I cannot take you through the Suez Canal. But tomorrow we will be in the Mediterranean Sea, nevertheless," said the captain.

"The Mediterranean!" I exclaimed. "You mean that you will go around the continent of Africa? Clear to the Cape of Good Hope and up through the Atlantic, the Straits of Gibraltar, and into the Mediterranean? Why, Captain, that is thousands of miles! How can you do that in one day?"

"We will pass beneath the Isthmus of Suez," he said.

"Beneath it? You mean that there is a passage beneath it?"

"Yes, there is. I call it the Arabian Tunnel. It goes beneath Suez, into the Mediterranean."

I stared at him. "But the Isthmus of Suez is made of shifting sand!"

"Fifty yards down there is solid rock. I reasoned out that there must be a passage. You see, I noticed the same kind of fish in both the Red Sea and in the Mediterranean. So I knew that there must be a tunnel between, which the fish knew about. Catching some of the fish, I put brass rings around their tails and threw them back into the Mediterranean. Some months later I caught some of the same fish on the coast of Syria. Thus I knew that there was an undersea tunnel. In *The Nautilus* I searched for it. Sure enough, I found it and dared to enter. Before long, Professor, you will pass through my Arabian Tunnel into the Mediterranean."

4 We Pass Through the Arabian Tunnel

We continued up the Red Sea into the Gulf of Suez. I plainly saw Mount Sinai, the high mountain, where the Bible says that God gave Moses the Ten Commandments.

By nightfall I could tell that we were very near Suez. Through the panel I could see the rock walls. I knew it would be a difficult passage. I knew that Captain Nemo himself would steer *The Nautilus* through the Arabian Tunnel.

To my surprise and delight, he asked me to sit with him in the pilot's cage. A cabin six feet square, it reminded me of the bridge of a Mississippi steamboat.

I watched him and the high, straight walls of coral in silence. It was about ten o'clock when he took the helm for our dangerous trip through the tunnel. A large opening, black and deep, was before us at last. A strange roaring was all around. It was the waters of the Red Sea rushing into the Mediterranean, which had a lower sea level.

Boldly the little *Nautilus* rushed into it, straight and fast as an arrow. My heart pounded as we rushed along.

After about thirty minutes Captain Nemo turned his head.

"We are in the Mediterranean Sea!" he said.

It was unbelievable! In only a few minutes, *The Nautilus* had passed under the Isthmus of Suez!

5 Ned Makes Plans to Escape

At seven o'clock next morning Ned joined me on the platform. He could hardly believe that we were in the Mediterranean Sea. He had slept through our exciting trip the night before, through the Arabian Tunnel.

"Now that we are once more in European waters," he said, "it is time to plan our escape. We must escape now, before Captain Nemo goes to the North Pole, or the South Pole. This may be our last chance."

I knew how much Ned wished to escape. For myself, though, I was in no hurry to end our voyage on *The Nautilus*. Thanks to Captain Nemo and our trip on his submarine, I was writing my book about undersea plants and animals right in the deep sea itself. I hated to think of leaving *The Nautilus* before my book was finished.

"Are you sorry that you came on this voyage?" I asked Ned.

"No, to be honest," he replied. "But now I want it ended."

"It will end some day. It has to," I told him.

"But where? When?" he asked.

"I don't know. I can't even guess. But I'd like another six months to finish my book before it ends."

"If Captain Nemo offered you freedom today, would you accept it?" he asked. "We may never have another chance, you know. If we are wise, we will escape the first chance we have."

"You win, Ned," I told him. "But remember one thing. We must be successful on our first attempt. If we fail, we'll never have another chance. You know that."

"That is true, whether we try to escape in two days or two years. But we must seize our first opportunity!"

"Yes, I agree," I told him. "What do you think is our best chance?"

"A dark night," Ned said, "and short distance from some seacoast in Europe. Even if we were underwater, I would try to seize the dinghy. I know how to sail it now. We'd have to get inside the control room and I can bring it to the surface. I've watched it done."

"Well, don't forget—one hitch will ruin us. But watch out for a chance. Do you know what I think?"

"No. What?"

"I think we won't have a chance at all. Captain Nemo knows we haven't given up thoughts of escape. He will be on his guard, now that we are near Europe."

"We shall see. He may have other things on his mind."

Was Captain Nemo suspicious? Or was he hiding from surface vessels? He kept far beneath the surface, at any rate, far from the shore. He was silent and busy.

One day an amazing thing happened. I was watching out the panel, when suddenly before my eyes a man appeared! He was a diver, carrying at his belt a leather bag. He flattened his face against the glass and looked in at us!

To my great amazement, Captain Nemo, who was beside me, made a sign to him. The diver made an answering motion and returned at once to the surface.

"Do not be alarmed," the captain said to us, "that is Nicholas, a bold diver in this part of the world."

"You know him?"

"Of course. Why not?"

Then Captain Nemo went to an iron chest which had an N on the top. He opened it. It was full of gold pieces, worth millions!

Where did all this gold come from, I wondered. How did Captain Nemo get it? What was he going to do with it? I watched him without a word as he fastened the lid and locked it. He wrote an address on it in Greek. Then he pressed a button.

Four men appeared and pushed the chest out of the room. I heard them take it up the iron staircase with pulleys.

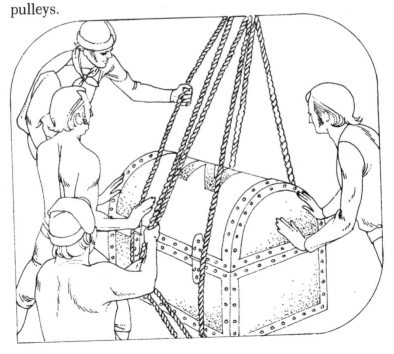

"Good night, Professor," said the captain, as he turned and left.

I returned to my room, but could not sleep, wondering what connection there was between the diver and the chest of gold. Soon I knew by our pitching and tossing that we were on the surface. Then I heard the dinghy being launched upon the water.

Two hours later it returned, and again we plunged under the water. Plainly the gold had been sent somewhere. Who received it? Why? I was very curious.

6 We Rush Through the Mediterranean

The Mediterranean is one of the most beautiful bodies of water in the world. It has one of the finest climates, too. But we scarcely saw it in our mad rush.

It was plain by now that Captain Nemo did not like the Mediterranean. Did it bring back unhappy memories? Did it have too many sorrows for him? Did he suspect that we would try to escape? Whatever the reason, we rushed along at a dizzy speed, unable to see even the fish accurately. I wished that we would go more slowly, but Captain Nemo did not even appear.

Ned, to his great displeasure, was obliged to forget his plans for escape. Going so fast, we could not launch a boat. It would be like jumping off a fast train.

On February 18, about three o'clock in the morning, we went through the Straits of Gibraltar and were in the Atlantic Ocean. Ned was in a black mood.

"Don't blame yourself," I told him. "It would have been foolish to try to escape. Don't give up. Maybe we are going up the coast of Portugal. France and England aren't far off. Let's just wait and see."

"Tonight we escape," he said in a low voice. "We will be on the surface, a few miles from the Spanish coast. It is cloudy. Tonight at nine o'clock, Captain Nemo will be in his room—he always is. The engineers and crew will not see us. I have put oars, mast, and sail into the dinghy. I even put in some food. I will wait for you at the central staircase. Everything is ready."

"But the sea is bad," I told him.

"We'll have to take that chance. The dinghy is strong. Only a few miles, and we are free. By eleven or midnight, we will be somewhere on land."

I had no time to think or speak. Then with a sick feeling I realized that at that very moment *The Nautilus* was sinking under the Atlantic Ocean!

I wanted to regain my freedom, I discovered, even if it meant leaving my underwater studies unfinished. No oath bound us to Captain Nemo. Perhaps we would be far away tomorrow. Then I felt a slight shock, and I knew we had settled on the bottom of the ocean.

"Ah, sir!" said Captain Nemo brightly, coming out of his door. "I have been looking for you. We are on the bottom of Vigo Bay!"

"Vigo Bay?" I asked, puzzled. "What is Vigo Bay? I do not know of it."

"On October 22, 1702, a convoy of twenty-three Spanish ships loaded with gold from America were sunk in Vigo Bay. All twenty-three ships went to the bottom with all their immense riches."

"Well?" I asked.

"We are in Vigo Bay. Would you like to see that vast treasure?"

He pointed to the window. I looked. For half a mile, the electric light made everything bright. The ship's crew in diving suits were gathering the gold. Loading themselves with their precious booty, the men returned to *The Nautilus*. When they had disposed of their load, they returned to the endless supply.

"Now you know where I get my millions," said Captain Nemo. "This wreck and a thousand others, all over the world, keep me supplied with wealth. All are known to me. All are marked on my submarine map."

"I pity the poor people who have lost this gold," I said. "And I pity the poor people who need this wealth but do not have it."

"Do you think that these riches are lost, just because I gather them?" he asked. "I do not collect these riches for myself. I make good use of them. I know that there are poor and oppressed people in the world. Do you understand?"

He stopped, and I saw that he was sorry he had said so much. Here was a man who felt sorry for suffering people everywhere.

Then I understood who would receive these millions. It was the poor and downtrodden. For them Captain Nemo and *The Nautilus* were cruising in the waters of the world.

7 *Again the Southern Cross*

Next morning Ned looked discouraged. He did not look up, and he barely spoke.

"Well, Ned," I said, "luck was against us yesterday."

"Yes. Captain Nemo went undersea—and at the very moment we planned to escape from the submarine. Who knows when we'll get another chance!"

"He had business at the bank."

"At the bank?"

"His undersea bank," I answered, "on the bottom of Vigo Bay."

Then I told him about our visit to the twenty-three sunken ships loaded with gold, on the bottom of Vigo Bay. Ned had been asleep all the time, so he knew nothing of our visit.

"Well, maybe we'll have better luck next time," he said, "if there is a next time. What direction are we going now?"

I looked at the chart.

"I hate to tell you, Ned. But we have left Europe far behind. We are 325 miles from the nearest land, headed south by southwest."

"I wonder where we are headed for," he muttered.

"Who knows? Weather is bad, too."

"Very bad—fog, wind, clouds, and rough seas. Not a ship has been in sight for many days now."

For several days we sailed on, with nothing to break

the monotony. I passed my time writing my book and looking out the side panels. I was never bored watching the underwater plants and animals. Fish in these waters were very large. I noticed sharks fifteen or twenty feet long. Swordfish nearly twenty-five feet in length were not uncommon.

On and on we went, in the Gulf Stream. Everyone knows about this tremendous current of clear, blue water in the Atlantic Ocean. Warmed by the sun in the Gulf of Mexico, it flows between Florida and Cuba, turning to the northeast. Then it splits in two. One current flows down the coast of Ireland and Norway. The other flows along Africa and back to the Gulf, where it started.

In the center of the Gulf Stream there is a quiet place called the Sargasso Sea. Visiting it in *The Nautilus,* we found it almost like a huge meadow, for it was full of a kind of seaweed called "sargazso" in Spanish. Many fish feed there, and I enjoyed watching them through the side panels.

We had gone 300 miles a day for the past three weeks. The way we were heading, it appeared that we were bound for the South Atlantic. I could not guess whether we would go around the tip of South America again and to the Pacific Ocean. Maybe, instead, we would round the tip of South Africa. Or, maybe, we would go to the South Pole.

The South Pole—that would be madness indeed! But I had no way of knowing what was in Captain Nemo's mind. I hardly saw him at all these days. When I did see him, he was either busy or silent.

Well, at any rate, nothing could be gained by our escaping now, I decided. And nothing would be gained by trying to seize the submarine. Still, I could see no use in asking Captain Nemo to let us go free. He would not do so—of that I was sure. It would only put him on his guard all the more. So I could see nothing to do but go along with *The Nautilus,* just as if we wanted to be there. But we must watch for another chance to escape.

Ned was silent these days. I seldom saw him, as he stayed in his room. But when I saw him, he had nothing to say. I could see that he was sick at heart, that he had been on *The Nautilus* much too long a time. It was almost more than he could bear. Rage burned in his eyes, and I was afraid he was on the point of doing some violent deed. I knew he was not angry with me, but he was in a very bad mood.

"How many men do you think there are on board *The Nautilus?*" he asked me.

"Oh, Ned, I can't even guess."

"Can't you estimate it? You know the size of the submarine, so you know how much air it holds. You know how much air a man breathes in twenty-four hours."

I could see what he was driving at.

"I see. Well, in a day a man breathes 634 gallons of air. *The Nautilus* contains—let me see— 396,300 gallons of air. Divide that by 634. *The Nautilus* has enough air for 625 men for twenty-four hours."

"Six hundred and twenty-five men!" he exclaimed. "But we know there aren't that many! We've never seen but a small part of that many men."

"I don't think there are. I've never seen them. Still, there may be more than just the two of us can handle."

Ned looked away. He shrugged his shoulders; then he turned and left the room without another word.

It was now March 14. We had come about thirteen

thousand leagues since we began our voyage off the coast of Japan on November 8, just four months before. Who could tell when it would end, or where?

For the second time since we left New York, we were in the Southern Hemisphere. Nightly I again watched the Southern Cross, when the weather was clear. I wondered how many more times we would cross the equator and sail under the beautiful rays of the Southern Cross before our voyage was ended.

8 The Iceberg at the South Pole

Farther we went, straight south. I kept wondering if Captain Nemo would really try to reach the South Pole. I hardly thought he would be so mad. Everyone else had failed in the attempt.

On March 16, I saw ice floating in the sea. Since the seasons are reversed south of the equator, March 16 would be the same as September 16 in the Northern Hemisphere.

More and more blocks of ice appeared as we continued south. They grew larger every day. Some of them were greenish, some yellow.

Finally our way was becoming almost blocked with ice. Captain Nemo would always find a narrow opening in the ice with some difficulty, and slip through it. It would close behind him. Often I thought, with a heavy heart, that we were prisoners of the icy seas. But guided by the captain's clever hand, we would slip through.

The temperature was now below zero. We wore seal or polar bear fur on the platform. Inside *The Nautilus,* however, electric heaters kept us comfortable.

Violent gales blew the snow, and always there were thick fogs and high seas.

At last, on March 18, we were definitely locked in the ice. All around us there was only endless ice. Icy mountains made a solid wall.

"What do you think of this?" demanded Ned. "Here we are—locked in the ice! Can you think of anything worse than this fix we are in? Is the captain crazy?"

"I think we are caught, all right," I answered. "Winter is too near for the ice to break up for many months. But I don't think the captain is crazy."

"I can see that you don't have much faith in *The Nautilus,*" said Captain Nemo, coming up just then. "You will see, though. We cannot only get out of this ice jam, but we can go still farther south."

"Farther south!" we exclaimed. "The Pole?"

"Yes. We are going to the South Pole. I thought you knew."

"To the Pole!" We could hardly believe our ears.

"That's right. You know, I can do almost anything in *The Nautilus.*"

We knew that Captain Nemo was bold and fearless. But wasn't this madness?

"No man has ever been to the South Pole!" I exclaimed. "All have failed!"

"That is correct. But we will discover it together—just think of that! Others have failed, but I will not fail. You will see!"

"Then why don't we go ahead?" I said crossly. "Let's smash through the ice barrier! Let's melt it! Let's blow it up! Let's fly over it!"

"Not over it, gentlemen," he said, calmly. "Under it!"

"Under it!"

Then I began to understand what he had in mind.

"Now we are beginning to understand each other, Professor," he said half smiling. "It would be impossible for an ordinary ship, of course, to sail under the ice barrier. But it will be easy for *The Nautilus*. You will see—we will go to the Pole."

"But what if the Pole is on land?" I asked. "Or what if it is in the solid ice? What then?"

"The chances are good that it is in the open sea," he said.

"But what about air? You don't know how large the ice field is."

"You are right. Our only difficulty will be going without air. It will be several days before we can go up for a new supply of air. Air is our biggest problem."

Preparations for our daring trip to the South Pole under the ice were now begun. We all wanted to succeed, for we knew it would be death if we did not.

The powerful electric pumps began storing air in the reserve tanks. The panels were closed. A dozen or more men with pickaxs broke the ice around the submarine.

By filling the water tanks, once we were free of the ice, we descended to 2,600 feet, where it was much warmer. At twenty-six knots we moved ahead toward the Pole. At that rate, we would reach the Pole in forty hours.

No fish were in these waters. Once we struck an iceberg overhead. Captain Nemo told us there were 3,000 feet of ice over our heads at that point. He pointed to the manometer, which measured our depth.

"You see," he said, "for one foot of ice above the sea, there are three feet below it. I can estimate the thickness of the ice over us by our depth in the water."

I hardly took my eyes off the manometer during this part of our voyage.

By and by the air grew stale. We should have renewed our air supply long ago from the reserve tanks. But we knew that we might need the air much worse later. Sleep was painful. My chest ached and my head felt heavy. My thoughts and dreams were troubled and stupid. I felt as if I could neither go to sleep nor stay awake.

Mile after mile, on we went under the ice. The air got worse and worse. I became dizzy and weak. I thought the night would never end.

Next morning I woke up with my lungs full of fresh air that was pouring into *The Nautilus*. I knew by our rocking that we were on the surface of the water once more. I heard a knock on the door of my cabin.

"Come in," I called, thinking it was Ned.

Captain Nemo entered and said: "Open water!"

9 *The South Pole*

I rushed to the platform. There was a long stretch of open sea, with only a few pieces of ice. A world of birds was in the air, and the sea was full of fish. It was thirty-seven degrees.

"Are we really at the South Pole?" I asked, scarcely believing it.

"I don't know exactly. At noon I will take our bearings, if the sun comes out."

At ten o'clock I helped launch the dinghy. We put some instruments into it. Captain Nemo, Ned, and I stepped into it. We rowed over to a strip of rocky land nearby. We touched on the shore. I stepped aside and bowed to the captain.

"Sir," I said, "to you belongs the honor of being the first man to set foot at the South Pole."

He stepped lightly onto the shore. Then he climbed the rocks and stood with his arms folded. He was silent, looking about him.

"I do not hesitate to step on land—this land," he said. "No person has ever been here before me."

I noticed some mosses and little plants on the ground. On the shore were a few purple seaweeds and a great many little shells.

The air was full of birds, making deafening cries. They flew all about us. Penguins soberly watched us, showing not the slightest fear. Of course, they had never seen people before, so their curiosity made them come close to us.

Albatrosses with a wingspan of about thirteen feet flew overhead. Several kinds of seals and walruses were on the shore also. They showed no fear either and did not run from us. Ned touched my arm and pointed to one little family.

The father seal was watching over the mother, who nursed a baby. Other young seals swam about nearby, excellent swimmers. I liked their beautiful, soft eyes. I could not have harmed one of them.

For two days we were unable to take our position by the sun because it was so foggy.

"If we can't see the sun tomorrow," I told Ned, "we must give up the whole idea, and we'll never know if we are at the Pole. Tomorrow is March 21, the equinox. The sun will disappear behind the horizon for another six months. The long polar night will set in."

"You are right," said Captain Nemo, "it is tomorrow or never."

Next day Captain Nemo and I went together, as Ned refused to go with us. His temper was getting worse, day by day.

We climbed a small mountain. I held the chronometer, my heart pounding with excitement. If the disappearance of one-half of the sun came at exactly twelve o'clock on the chronometer, we were at the South Pole. We watched. Finally the sun appeared through a break in the fog. I looked at the chronometer.

"Twelve o'clock," I said.

"The South Pole!" replied Captain Nemo.

He rested his hand on my shoulder and spoke quietly.

"I, Captain Nemo, on this twenty-first day of March, 1868, have reached the South Pole. I take possession of this part of the globe."

"In whose name, Captain?" I asked.

"In my own, sir," he answered.

Captain Nemo unfurled a black banner. The letter N was handsomely decorated in gold upon it. Proudly it waved in the stiff breeze, a beautiful sight.

"Good-by, proud sun!" he said. "Disappear! Rest beneath this sea for half a year! Let a night that is six months long spread its shadows over my new domain!"

10 An Accident This Time

Early the next morning, we began preparations to leave the South Pole. It was intensely cold—nine degrees above zero. A bitter wind was blowing.

What becomes of the whales? I wondered. Where do they go for half of the year, when the Pole is frozen over? I wondered what warmer regions they inhabit. Like birds, they must go to more pleasant climates. Seals and walruses, I knew, break holes in the ice. They come up for air through these holes, which they keep open. They alone of the polar animals are not driven out by the cold.

The reservoirs of *The Nautilus* were filled with water. Slowly we began to descend into the ocean. At 1,000 feet we stopped descending and started forward at fifteen knots. Soon we were under an immense iceberg.

About three in the morning I was awakened by a violent shock which threw me onto the middle of the floor. I groped about to find the light. Pictures were hanging straight out from the wall, instead of straight down. I was walking on the wall, instead of the floor. *The Nautilus*, plainly, had been thrown on its side. Ned came in.

We went to the instrument room and looked at the manometer. It showed a depth of 1,180 feet. In a few minutes, Captain Nemo entered, looking worried. He

watched the instruments silently. I could not tell what he was thinking.

"An incident, Captain?" I asked. I remembered when we went aground on the coral reef in Torres Strait.

"No, sir. We have an accident this time," he said.

"A serious accident?"

"Perhaps."

"Is the danger immediate?"

"No, I think not."

"Is *The Nautilus* stranded?"

"Yes. An enormous block of ice—a whole mountain—has turned over. It struck *The Nautilus* and threw us over. You see, we are lying on our side."

"Can we right the ship by emptying the reservoirs?"

"We are doing that now, Professor. You can hear the pumps working. We are rising, as you can see." He did not take his eyes off the manometer.

Slowly *The Nautilus* returned to position. The pictures once more hung against the wall. The floor became horizontal again, and the walls were upright.

On either side of the submarine there was a wall of ice. First, we tried going ahead, but our way was blocked. Then we tried going back, but we were blocked again.

Plainly, we were enclosed in a tunnel of ice about twenty yards wide. The iceberg lay on top of the tunnel, and both ends were blocked.

11 Lack of Air

Thus, around *The Nautilus*—above, below, at both ends—our tunnel was closed with ice. We were prisoners of the iceberg.

"Gentlemen," said Captain Nemo, "there are two ways for us to die. We will not die of hunger, for our food will last longer than we do. Our first choice is to be crushed. The second is to die of suffocation. Shall we discuss it?"

"Are the air reservoirs full?" I asked.

"They hold air for forty-eight hours longer."

"Can we get out in forty-eight hours?"

"We will try it. We have to try to pierce the ice around us. Sound will tell which side is thinner. But we are in serious danger, and I rely on your bravery and your help."

"Sir," said Ned, "I will do anything I can. I am as handy with a pickax as a harpoon. Just tell me what to do."

At noon Ned and a dozen others were dressed in their cork jackets. With Captain Nemo they dug into the ice walls, taking soundings. The ceiling, they learned, was 1,300 feet thick, but below it was only 30 feet. That was the place to dig. We must move 230,000 cubic feet of ice before we would be free.

Instantly the men fell to work. In two hours they were replaced by a fresh crew, of which I was one. The water was very cold, but I soon got warm, chopping.

121

We worked under the water, with diving tanks on our backs. Our air was better than in *The Nautilus*, which was now very heavy from the long hours undersea.

Twelve hours of digging showed that it would take five nights and four days to dig out of the ice. Five nights and four days—but we had air for only two days—unless something happened! Were we going to die in this ice barrier? Our situation was bad.

Every man knew how hopeless our chances were. All were determined, however, to do their duty to the last. We worked by turns all night. We hated to return to the submarine, the air was so bad. Captain Nemo let in a little air from the tanks, however.

It looked to me like a losing fight. The water froze over as fast as we could dig the ice out. After tomorrow our air reservoirs would be empty. A cold sweat came over me. For five days we had lived on the air reserve on board. Now the air must be used by workers only. Even yet, as I write, my memory is so strong that terror seizes me. My lungs seemed to be without air, and my chest bursting.

"Boiling water—that is the answer!" shouted Captain Nemo. "Jets of boiling water will delay the freezing over!"

The heat was turned on full force. In a few minutes the water was boiling, and in three hours we had raised the temperature two degrees; in several more hours, another four degrees. It would indeed delay the freezing!

"We shall not be frozen in, at any rate," I said hopefully.

By the next day seventeen feet of ice had been cut away, and only thirteen remaining. Still, that would take forty-eight hours of work. The air in *The Nautilus* now could not be renewed. This day would make it worse. My lungs ached and burned as I breathed the poisoned air, and I was almost unconscious. We all acted half asleep.

Inside *The Nautilus* it was almost unbearable now. We gladly put on our cork jackets and went to work, though our hands were torn. At least, working we could breathe! By the end of that day, only six feet were left. Only six feet separated us now from escape. The reservoirs were all but empty. The little air that remained must be for the workers. Not a particle could be spared for *The Nautilus*.

I know not how to describe it. I breathed heavily now. My head ached, and I was dizzy, almost drunk. All the others were too. Some of them rattled as they breathed.

On the sixth day of our imprisonment, Captain Nemo decided to crush the remaining ice. *The Nautilus* was floated over the remaining thin ice, less than three feet thick. It had been bored with a thousand holes.

Then the reservoirs were opened. Soon 3,500 cubic feet of water were let in, to increase our weight 220,000 pounds. We were all locked into *The Nautilus*. We waited and listened. Soon I heard the roaring and cracking noise as we settled down and broke through the ice. Then *The Nautilus*, free of her prison, sank into the sea!

"We are off!" Ned cried.

I scarcely heard the yell. I was almost unconscious.

The Nautilus sank like a bullet. Then the electric pumps began to let water out of the tanks. Our fall was stopped. Soon we were moving ahead, the engine going at full speed. Trembling in every bolt, the sturdy little

Nautilus plunged steadily ahead toward the north. But how could we live another day without air?

At last I knew I was suffocating. I was stretched out across the bed, my face purple. I could not see or hear. All but dead, all notion of time had left my mind.

Where was Captain Nemo? I wondered. Had he died?

The Nautilus tore ahead at a frightful pace. The manometer showed that there were twenty feet of ice now between us and the open sea. Could we break it? We would try!

Now the stern was lowered to attacking position.

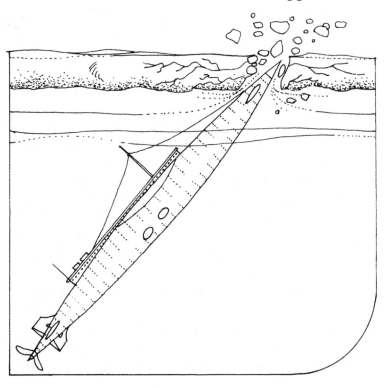

Suddenly, like a battering ram, *The Nautilus* attacked the ice barrier from below. It backed up. It rushed forward. It backed up again. It rushed forward—the second attempt we shot through the ice!

Instantly the panels were opened. Fresh, pure air rushed in to all parts of *The Nautilus*.

12 From Cape Horn to the Amazon

I breathed deeply, again and again, the life-giving sea air. Almost drunk with it, the men revived quickly. Now there was no need to be saving of air. Just to breathe filled us with delight.

"Ah," said Ned, opening his jaws wide enough to frighten a shark, "there is air enough for everybody now. I never knew it was so good just to breathe!"

"How did I get up here, Ned?" I asked. We were on the platform. "Did you carry me?"

"It wasn't much. You are not heavy, and I am strong. Look at these muscles!"

"Ned, good friend, I am bound to you for life. I am under a great debt to you."

"Well, if you are bound to me, I suppose I have the right to take you with me when I leave."

"Let's see where we are going first, before we talk of escape," I said.

The Nautilus went at a rapid rate. Soon out of the Antarctic Circle, we began to think once more of the future, instead of our horrible experience at the South Pole.

We were heading north into the Atlantic. Soon we sighted Tierra del Fuego, named by the sailors for the smoke rising from huts on the island. There began to be more seaweed now, and many geese and ducks.

For days Captain Nemo did not appear. Following the winding coast of South America, we stayed well out to sea. The coasts of Brazil we passed at a flying pace. Ned was, of course, on the watch again for a chance to escape, but he saw none.

On April 11 we came to the surface of the ocean near the mouth of the Amazon River. Its mouth is so vast that one can still find fresh water several leagues out to sea. Then we crossed the equator. Ned talked some of escaping to French Guiana, but a stiff wind was blowing. In the mountainous waves we could not have launched our dinghy. Escape was plainly impossible. We must try only when we had a fair chance to succeed.

I passed my time studying. Working on my book was my interest and pleasure, and many plants and animals were in these waters.

We saw several groups of sea cows, or manatees. These beautiful, peaceful animals grow to be from twenty to twenty-five feet long, and weigh up to 9,000 pounds.

"Nature gave an important job to these animals," I told Ned. "They eat plants only. Their work is to keep the shores and rivers clear of weeds and rushes."

"But they have been almost all killed—haven't they?" he asked.

"Yes, this useful animal has almost disappeared. And so the rivers and shores fill up with weeds. The stagnant water breeds yellow fever mosquitoes. The balance of nature has been upset. The seals and whales keep diseases down also."

Paying no attention to me, however, the crew took six manatees for food. They taste excellent, much like beef. We also caught fish and turtles on the shores of the Amazon River. By nightfall we were again at sea.

13 The Octopus Fight

Ned was now counting on escape in the Gulf of Mexico. We would swim to land, if the submarine was close enough. Or we would hail a boat, if we saw one. Or we would launch the dinghy, if we had a chance fairly close to land.

For six months we had been prisoners in *The Nautilus*. We had traveled 17,000 leagues. We could hope for nothing from Captain Nemo, and must depend on ourselves alone.

For several days I had not seen Captain Nemo. He seemed to be avoiding me. He was more withdrawn and less sociable. I wondered why he had changed so much.

I wanted to escape. But I wanted also to take the notes for my book. Now I had material for the true book of the deep sea. I wanted my book to be published, not lost in the ocean. Each day, watching through the panels, I took more notes.

By April 20 we were off the Bahamas. I saw the submarine caves in the rocks there, in shallow water. I showed them to Ned.

"Those are exactly the places to look for octopuses," I said. "It would not surprise me to see some of these monsters."

"Do you mean the ordinary octopus?" he asked.

129

"No, the huge ones."

"Oh, I remember perfectly. Once I saw a large ship pulled under the waves by a huge octopus," he said.

"What! You saw that?" I asked.

"Yes, I saw it."

"With your own eyes?" I could not believe him.

"Certainly. With my own eyes."

"Where did that happen?" I asked.

"At Saint-Malo, my hometown in France."

"In the harbor?"

"No, in a church," he replied.

"In a church! Are you insane?"

"In a church there is a picture of an octopus pulling a ship under the water."

"Oh, Ned! When will I ever learn when you are joking?" We both laughed.

I was glad that he felt like joking again, for I knew he was happier. Looking forward again to a chance to escape was good for his spirits.

"Oh, I have heard of that picture," I said. "It is only a legend though, not true. It is pure imagination. People used to believe the most impossible things about the octopus."

"How large does an octopus get?" he asked.

"Oh, it is seldom more than six feet across."

"Well," he said calmly, pointing out the panel, "here is one larger than that now."

I looked. Before my eyes was a horrible monster twenty-five feet long! It swam backwards toward us with great speed, watching us with enormous, staring blue-green eyes. Its eight arms, or rather legs, fixed to its head, were twisted like snakes. I could see at least 250 suckers on the underside of its tentacles. It had a horned beak, like a parakeet's. In color it changed from gray to brown. What a monster it was! I took my pencil and began to draw it.

Soon more of the hideous creatures came. I counted seven. Suddenly we stopped.

In a minute Captain Nemo entered. I had not seen him for many days. He looked out the panel and said something to his lieutenant. Soon the panels closed.

"A curious collection of octopuses," I said to him.

"Yes indeed. We are going to fight them hand to hand."

"Man to beast?"

"Yes. The propeller is stopped. I think one is tangled in it. That is what stopped us. We will slaughter them."

"Ned and I will go with you," I said, and we followed him.

About ten of us took axes, and Ned took his faithful harpoon. Hardly was the panel open when one of the arms of an octopus slid like a snake down the opening. With one blow Captain Nemo cut the arm off with his ax. It slid, wriggling down the ladder.

Two other arms lashed the air and reached down the ladder. They seized the man just above Captain Nemo, lifting him up. What a scene! The uphappy man was balanced high in the air, yelling with terror.

"Help! Oh, help!" he screamed in French.

To hear my native language uttered in such a frightful situation startled me. I had a countryman on board, maybe several! That heart-piercing scream! I shall hear it all of my life. The unfortunate man—who could rescue him?

Captain Nemo rushed up and cut off one arm of the

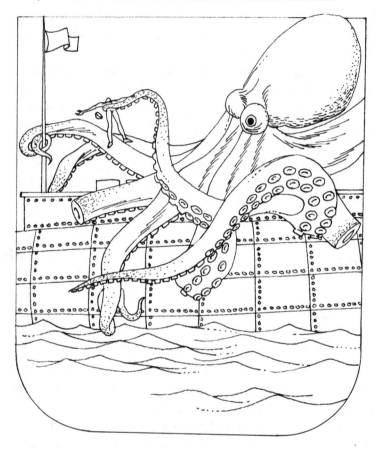

octopus. The crew fought it with axes. Ned and I also buried our weapons in the beast.

For an instant I thought we had saved the man. Seven of the creature's eight arms had been cut off. Only one arm now held the man. Just as Captain Nemo and his lieutenants threw themselves on it, the octopus squirted a stream of inky liquid. We were blinded.

When we had wiped our eyes, the octopus had disappeared with my poor countryman.

Ten or twelve of the animals now crawled over *The Nautilus*. We fought pell-mell with this nest of serpents. They wriggled on the platform in waves of slippery blood and ink. Suddenly Ned Land was knocked off his feet. I rushed to help him. But Captain Nemo was there before me. His ax disappeared in a beast's head. Then Ned, one arm free, plunged his harpoon deep into the heart of the octopus.

The monsters, beaten and cut to pieces, left at last, disappearing under the waves. Captain Nemo, covered with blood and nearly exhausted, gazed upon the sea that had swallowed one of his faithful men. His face was a picture of grief and misery.

I shall never forget that terrible scene on April 20. The captain's sorrow was great. Two companions he had lost since our arrival on *The Nautilus*. And what a death this poor man had! Crushed, bruised, and drowned by the dreadful creature, he could never rest in the coral cemetery beside his friends.

But it was the despairing scream of the man in his last agony that tore my heart. The poor man, forgetting submarine language in his death agony, had remembered only his mother tongue. Here on the submarine, all this time I had a countryman but did not know it. He was a rebel against man, like Captain Nemo. Was he the only Frenchman on board? I could not help wondering.

Again, I did not see Captain Nemo for days. With no one at the helm, motionless, *The Nautilus* floated about like a corpse.

14 Back in the Gulf Stream

Resuming our northerly course after some days, we were once more in sight of the Bahamas. Now we were back in the Gulf Stream, the largest ocean current. It has its own banks, its own fish, and its own temperature, besides its own water. It is really a blue river in the sea, and its waters do not mix with the ocean.

I saw an amazingly curious variety of fish in the Gulf Stream. They were very interesting to study. The bright, phosphorescent waters delighted me too.

On May 8 we were near Cape Hatteras, near the coast of North Carolina. Ned and I thought we might be able to escape along this coast, which was only thirty miles off. Many steamers went up and down between New York or Boston and the Gulf of Mexico. We could hope to be picked up. One serious difficulty, however, was the bad weather, for it was the season of hurricanes. In these heavy seas the little boat was certain of destruction. Even Ned admitted this, eager as he was to escape.

"Professor," he said one day, "I can stand it no longer. I had enough at the South Pole. I will not go to the North Pole, if that is what Captain Nemo plans to do next."

"Still, there is no use of jumping into the sea, to certain death," I said.

"I would rather throw myself into the sea than go on like this," he said. "Before long we will be off Nova

Scotia. The St. Lawrence is my river. Quebec is my hometown. I would rather die than go on past."

Plainly Ned had indeed reached the end of his patience. I wanted to get off *The Nautilus* myself. Nearly seven months had passed with no news from our homeland. Captain Nemo's isolation put an end to my enthusiasm.

"Do you want me to ask Captain Nemo to let us go?"

"Yes, by all means. If you do not, then I intend to myself," he said.

I went to Captain Nemo's room and knocked at the door. No answer. I knocked again and turned the handle of the door. It opened, so I entered. Captain Nemo was there. He raised his head and frowned when he saw me.

"You here! I did not tell you to come in. What do you want?" he asked rudely.

"I would like to speak to you, Captain."

"But I am busy. I let you work in peace. Can't you do the same for me?"

"Sir, I have to speak to you at once. It is important."

"What is it then?"

"Will you give us our liberty?"

"Liberty?"

"Yes, sir. That is what I came to talk about. For seven months we have been on *The Nautilus*. Do you intend to keep us here forever?"

"Professor, my answer is the same as seven months ago. Whoever enters *The Nautilus* must never leave it."

"But that is slavery! Even a slave has a right to seek freedom!"

"That is true, but what of it?"

"Captain, I am not asking for myself. I like to study here. I can forget everything. But Ned Land is different from me."

"I did not ask Ned Land to come on board. I do not ask him to stay. I have nothing more to say to you. Let this be the last time you come to discuss this matter with me. Next time I will not listen."

I went to tell Ned about my conversation with the captain.

"Well, we know that we can expect nothing from him. Now we are nearing Long Island. There we will escape, whatever the weather."

But the storm which had followed us up the coast grew worse daily. A hurricane was following us. The air was white and misty, with low clouds rushing by. The angry sea rose in huge billows, and the barometer was extremely low.

Finally the storm hit on May 8, just as we came to Long Island, a few miles from New York Harbor. Captain Nemo decided to ride out the storm on the surface. He lashed himself to the platform. I did the same. It was thrilling to watch the storm rage, with that admirable man in the teeth of it.

Sometimes *The Nautilus* lay on its side tossing. Sometimes it stood on end, rolling and pitching. About five o'clock a torrent of rain fell that would overturn houses, break iron gates, or do any destruction. However, *The Nautilus,* a steel spindle, braved its fury unhurt.

I watched the raging waves. They were up to 50 feet high and 500 to 600 feet long. Their speed was thirty-five miles per hour. Such waves can destroy whole towns.

The height of the storm's fury was in the night. The

sky was on fire with lightning. The air was full of deafening noise made by howling waves, roaring wind, and crashing thunder. The wind seemed to blow from all directions at once.

Crushed and weak from the hours out in the magnificent storm, I crawled to the panel during a lull in the blast. It was impossible to stand upright in *The Nautilus*. It was midnight. I heard the reservoirs filling.

Slowly *The Nautilus* sank beneath the waves. Before we could find quiet, we had to go down to 150 feet. But there it was silent and peaceful. It was hard to believe that there was a hurricane loose upon the surface. Exhausted, I fell asleep.

15 *Our Situation Grows Worse*

The tropical hurricane blew us far off our course. All hope of escape to Long Island or to the mouth of the St. Lawrence had disappeared. Poor Ned shut himself away in despair.

For some days we wandered in a dense fog off Labrador. What accidents are due to these thick fogs! What collisions between vessels, in spite of warning bells, foghorns, lights, and whistles!

On May 15 we were south of the Grand Banks. Here the warm Gulf Stream from the south meets the icy Arctic current coming down from the north. Fog and icebergs are a great danger to ships.

Two days later, at a depth of 9,000 feet, I saw the transatlantic cable lying on the bottom of the sea. As I looked at it, crusted with shells, I thought of the two attempts, in 1857 and 1863, that had failed to lay the cable across the Atlantic. But then, in 1866, Cyrus Field, the American, sank all his fortune in a third cable, which was a success.

Was Captain Nemo going to the British Isles? I wondered. To my surprise, however, he circled Ireland and passed south to Land's End. *The Nautilus* was going in large circles now. Evidently we were looking for something.

I watched the captain one day, as he was looking out to sea. A vessel was actually putting on steam,

coming toward us. It was about six miles away when I
sighted it. At that very moment a dull boom came over
the waves. Ned Land came running up.

"Was that a gunshot?" he yelled.

I pointed in the direction of the vessel.

"I hope it is a warship!" he said. "I hope it reaches
us and sinks this cursed *Nautilus*."

We stood and watched the ship steaming toward
us, a large armored warship.

"If that ship comes within a mile of us, I shall
throw myself into the sea. I advise you to do the same,"
said Ned.

"And what if Captain Nemo then sinks the ship,
even if it takes time to haul us out of the sea?" I asked.

Presently a white puff of smoke burst from the
guns on her deck. Seconds later a loud explosion struck
my ear at the stern of *The Nautilus*.

"They are shooting at us!" I yelled.

"Doubtless they have recognized *The Nautilus*."

"But surely they can see that we are men!" I said.

"That is probably the very reason they are firing at
us," he said.

Now I could understand many things. No doubt on
every ocean ships were seeking this submarine we were
on, as the *Abraham Lincoln* had been. The *Abraham
Lincoln* had doubtless got to port and reported seeing
The Nautilus. This ship did not know who Ned and I
were. Had Captain Nemo decided to take revenge now on
the world? Prisoners, Ned and I would be killed, we
who only wanted to escape.

Had Captain Nemo not attacked some vessel in the
Indian Ocean, when the man was killed whom we buried
in the coral cemetery? It must be so! Now all nations

were united in hunting Captain Nemo, the enemy of all the world.

It was now plain. Instead of friends on the rescuing ship we saw coming, there were enemies hunting *The Nautilus.* And Ned and I, the innocent, would suffer too.

Shots rattled above. Some struck the sea, but none touched *The Nautilus.*

"Pierre, we must do all we can to get off this cursed submarine. Let's signal them! Maybe they will understand that we are not enemies," Ned said.

Ned took his handkerchief to wave in the air. He scarcely had it out of his pocket when an iron hand struck him. He fell, in spite of his strength, flat upon the deck.

"Fool!" exclaimed Captain Nemo. "Do you want me to kill you?"

Captain Nemo was terrible to see and to hear. Deadly pale, he roared at us and shook Ned by the shoulders. Turning to the approaching ship, he shook his fist at them and yelled.

"Ah, ship of a cursed nation, you know who I am! And I know you! Look, here are my colors!"

Captain Nemo unfurled a black flag like the one he had placed at the South Pole. Its black background brought out the letter *N* embroidered in gold.

"Now, Professor, you and Mr. Land go down below. Go now."

"Are you going to attack this ship?"

"Yes, I am going to sink it."

"You would not do that!" I said.

"I shall do it!" he replied coldly. "Keep your opinions to yourself. Fate has showed you what you never should have seen. The attack has already begun. Go below!"

"What is this vessel?" I asked.

"You don't know? Well, so much the better."

We went below, as ordered. We could do nothing else. About fifteen sailors stood around the captain, watching the approaching ship with hate. The engine was set in motion, and soon *The Nautilus* was out of reach of the guns of the approaching ship.

All that day, all that night, the chase went on. Finally steps were taken that meant action. The iron railing around the platform was lowered. The pilot cage was taken inside *The Nautilus*, flush with the deck.

"Ned, my friend," I said, "may God protect us!"

I was so nervous I knew not what to do. A hissing noise told me that water was running into the reservoirs. In a few minutes, *The Nautilus* began to sink. I understood. Captain Nemo was going to strike below the water line, where the wooden planks were not shielded with metal. He was lowering the submarine into striking position.

Again we were unwilling prisoners, witnesses of a dreadful scene. We took refuge in my room to wait; we could not speak. My mind stood still as I listened. Suddenly our speed increased—we were rushing. The whole ship trembled and shook. I let out a cry.

I felt the shock of the blow. I felt the steel spur tear, rattle, scrape. *The Nautilus*, driven by powerful motors, pierced the side of the ship, cutting through, like a needle through canvas! Ned and I were knocked to the floor.

I could stand it no longer. Getting to my feet, I rushed out of the room. Captain Nemo, silent and

gloomy, was looking through the panel. I looked too.

The ship was sinking into the water beside us. *The Nautilus* was going down beside it, into the depths. Thirty feet off I saw the open hole through which the water was pouring. The bridge was covered with moving men.

The poor men, terror stricken, were crowding the ratlines, clinging to the masts, struggling in the water. I was paralyzed with fright, stiff with anguish. My hair stood on end, my eyes stared. Panting for breath, without voice, I stood and watched their sufferings, glued to the glass in fright.

Suddenly there was an explosion. The decks blew up. Then the unfortunate ship sank quickly. Soon it disappeared with its dead crew, drawn down by the depths of the sea.

I turned to Captain Nemo. That terrible man of revenge, the man of hatred, was still watching the wreck. When it had disappeared, he turned. He opened the door of his room and entered. On the wall of his room I noticed the portrait of a woman still young. With her were two little children, very beautiful.

Captain Nemo stood looking at them for some minutes. Then he stretched his arms out toward them. He sank to his knees and burst into sobs.

16 The Last Words of Captain Nemo

The panels were now closed. *The Nautilus* was entirely dark as we left the location of the dreadful wreck of the battleship.

We were speeding through the fog, bound for northern seas. Back in my room, I could not sleep for nightmares. Daytime was filled with a great horror of Captain Nemo. I could not get him out of my mind. Whatever had happened to him in the past, I felt, he had no right to take such revenge upon the world.

Since the clocks on board had all stopped, I had no idea what time it was. I lost all track of the days. How long our voyage on *The Nautilus* would have lasted, I do not know. But a catastrophe finally occurred which ended it very suddenly.

I had not seen Captain Nemo or any of the crew since the wreck. I had not seen Ned.

Ned's hope of escape, I knew, was now gone. I knew that he must be in despair. I was afraid that, all hope gone, he would kill himself.

One night I had fallen into a heavy sleep. Suddenly I woke up. Ned, shaking my shoulder, was standing over me.

"Come on, Pierre," he whispered, "we are going to escape—now!"

"Where are we?"

"In sight of land about twenty miles to the east. On the surface."

144

"What country is it?"

"I don't know. But whatever country it is, it is better than *The Nautilus*."

"Is the weather still bad?"

"Quite bad. The sea is heavy. The wind is violent."

"Do you think we can make it to shore?"

"We can make it to land in the dinghy. I slipped out the oars and some food. No one is around."

"All right, Ned. You can count on me." I started pulling on my clothes.

"The moon rises late tonight, and it is cloudy anyway. That is a good thing. Hurry!"

"Where will I meet you? And when? I want to gather up my book notes."

"Meet me at the dinghy on deck, in an hour. Ten o'clock. I'll wait for you there. Put on warm clothes, for it is cold. If anyone discovers us, I'll kill—"

"We will die together, Ned!" We shook hands and he left.

I went to the instrument room. I saw that our course was north-northeast. Then I went back to dress for our escape. I put on heavy, warm clothing. With shaking hands, I collected all the notes for my book. I put them carefully in the inside pockets of my coat, next to my body for protection.

My heart beat loudly. I stretched out on the bed to quiet my shaking body. Again, I saw all my life on *The Nautilus*. Everything that had happened went through my mind. I remembered the night we came on board as prisoners. I thought of the submarine hunt on Crespo Island and being grounded on the coral reef in the Torres Strait. Our escape from the savages went through my mind, and the funeral in the coral cemetery. I recalled our trip under the Suez, the Indian pearl diver off Ceylon, and our visit to the undersea bank in Vigo Bay. Our trip to the South Pole came to my mind, the octopus fight in the Bahamas, and the hurricane.

Above all, I remembered ramming and sinking the warship with all her crew clinging to the ratlines. All of these things flew through my mind. Captain Nemo haunted me. He seemed to be the evil spirit of the world, living in the sea from which we were trying to escape. It was now 9:30. I closed my eyes.

There was another half hour to wait, another half hour of agony. Suddenly I heard the organ in the lounge playing a sad, wailing song that filled the air. It was wildly beautiful.

When it was almost ten, I left my room. I opened the lounge door softly, crept along the carpet with my heart pounding, avoiding the slightest noise.

Suddenly, as I reached the exit door, Captain Nemo got up. I froze. He came toward me, gliding like a ghost, silent, staring straight ahead and not seeing me at all. He was sobbing.

"Almighty God!" I heard him murmur. "Enough! Enough!" These were the last words I heard him say.

I rushed up the staircase. Creeping through the opening, I reached the boat. Ned was there waiting for me.

"Let's get out of here!" I whispered.

We closed the trapdoor silently behind us.

"You loosen the bolts in that end of the dinghy," Ned said, handing me a wrench. "I'll loosen this end. Hurry!"

We stepped into the boat and began to unscrew the bolts that held it.

"What was that noise? Listen!" said Ned.

Below, inside *The Nautilus*, there was a sudden loud yelling of many men. I shook so that I could hardly hold the wrench.

"They must have discovered that we are gone," I said.

"Then they'll be after us. Here is a dagger," he said, slipping it into my hand in the dark. "Use it! Kill whoever comes through that door!"

"Wait, Ned! Listen! I think—what are they saying?"

I listened again. One word, I noticed, was repeated over and over by the men yelling below. "The Maelstrom! The Maelstrom!"

"The Maelstrom!" we cried.

The Maelstrom! Could a more dreadful word have been thought of at a more dreadful time and place!

Now I knew why the crew was excited. It was not because they had discovered our absence. They were not looking for us at all. They were yelling because *The Nautilus* was caught in that dreadful whirlpool known as the Maelstrom!

Now I knew exactly where we were. We were near the coast of Norway. To be sure, we were being sucked into the huge, dangerous whirlpool that is the nightmare of all seafaring men. It is ten miles each way from the center of the Maelstrom, the largest whirlpool in the world.

At the very moment of leaving *The Nautilus* forever, we discovered that we were about to launch our dinghy in the terrible Maelstrom! In another three minutes, we would have been helpless in its sucking current. There was no time to think.

The Nautilus was indeed going around in a circle.

Our dinghy, still bolted to the platform, though with loosened bolts, was carried along at a dizzy speed. *The Nautilus* might survive the Maelstrom, but how could our little boat?

Sick with dread and fear, I was covered with sweat in the chilly night.

What a noise! The roaring and rushing of water were deafening. *The Nautilus* rocked frightfully. Its steel sides groaned and cracked. Sometimes Ned and I seemed to be standing upright in the little boat.

"Hold on!" we yelled to each other.

We heard a loud crash as the loosened bolts gave way that held us to the deck. The dinghy, torn from the platform, shot like a stone right into the middle of the Maelstrom!

My head struck an iron rib with a violent blow. I lost consciousness.

Conclusion

Thus ends our voyage under the sea for 20,000 leagues in *The Nautilus*.

The next thing I knew, I was lying on a bed in a fisherman's hut. Ned, safe and sound, was on the floor on his knees beside me. He was drying out the pages of my book, which were spread all over the floor. He stood up and smiled at me. Then he came to the bed.

"My book?" I asked, clasping his hand. "Is it all here?"

"Not one page is missing," he smiled. "But you can see that it is not a dry book. And it is full of the sea."

Good old Ned and his jokes. We laughed together and fell to talking.

"Where are we?" I asked.

"We are in the Lofoten Islands, off the coast of Norway," he told me. "A steamship comes here only once a month. On the next trip we will go back to France. I have made arrangements."

"Good," I said.

I went back to sleep. I rested for several more days and grew stronger.

Here, among the good people of the fishing village who pulled us out of the sea, I have spent my time writing this book about our adventures on *The Nautilus*. I have left out nothing, changed nothing. I have told the whole truth about our trip.

I do not know what happened to *The Nautilus*. I wonder if it stood the pressure of the Maelstrom. Some day, I know, there will be another *Nautilus*. Science and progress will build one.

Does Captain Nemo still live? [1] Does he still follow the ocean? Or did he mean, in his last words, that he was sorry? Had his agony of conscience broken his iron will? Or did he mean that he had enough of the sea?

If Captain Nemo still lives, I hope the hatred is gone from his savage heart. I hope the wonders in the sea will wash away his spirit of revenge. May he, wise thinker that he is, continue to explore the secrets of the sea. May he be at peace with himself and with the world!

[1] In *The Mysterious Island*, Jules Verne tells what happened to Captain Nemo and *The Nautilus*.

REVIEWING YOUR READING

PART I

CHAPTER 1

FINDING THE MAIN IDEA

1. In this chapter the narrator is mainly interested in the question:
   (A) Where are we going?   (B) Why are we going?
   (C) What are we looking for?   (D) Who are we?

REMEMBERING DETAIL

2. The journey of the *Abraham Lincoln* begins in
   (A) the South Seas   (B) the Atlantic Ocean   (C) the Pacific Ocean   (D) the Arctic Ocean
3. Ships at sea had been observing the mysterious object for several
   (A) days   (B) weeks   (C) months   (D) years
4. All of the following were true of the mysterious object EXCEPT that it
   (A) was smaller than a whale   (B) spouted water
   (C) seemed to glow   (D) was faster than the ship
5. Ned Land was hired on the ship as a
   (A) navigator   (B) harpooner   (C) cabin boy
   (D) captain

DRAWING CONCLUSIONS

6. In this chapter the narrator gets to know the men on the ship by
   (A) reading their mail   (B) asking them questions
   (C) arguing with them   (D) listening to them
7. You can figure out that the reason the crew was sitting in the rigging of the ship was because
   (A) it was very comfortable there   (B) they might see the creature from there   (C) they enjoyed being very high up
   (D) the captain told them to

USING YOUR REASON

8. In this chapter the crew listened to Ned Land's opinion mainly because he
   (A) had a lot of experience   (B) was about forty
   (C) had seen the creature   (D) was a good storyteller

IDENTIFYING THE MOOD

9. At this point in the story the crew is mostly feeling
   (A) fear   (B) anger   (C) sadness   (D) excitement

READING FOR DEEPER MEANING

10. Ned Land would most agree with which of the following?
    (A) Better safe than sorry.   (B) Luck is where you find it.
    (C) Seeing is believing.   (D) Curiosity killed the cat.

THINKING IT OVER

1. The narrator thinks that the cabin boy is "clever for his age."
   What information is provided in this chapter to prove that
   statement?
2. In this chapter there is more than one mystery. Although we
   are introduced to several characters, the narrator does not tell
   us anything about himself. Who do you think he is? What
   kind of person? What do you think he is doing on the ship?
   Why?

CHAPTER 2

FINDING THE MAIN IDEA

1. In this chapter Ned Land and the narrator mostly discuss
   (A) politics   (B) their past life   (C) the weather
   (D) the sea monster

REMEMBERING DETAIL

2. The narrator of the book is a
   (A) farmer   (B) cook   (C) science teacher
   (D) carpenter's helper
3. The narrator's name is
   (A) Bill   (B) José   (C) Pierre   (D) Sol
4. How long is the sea monster said to be?
   (A) 50 feet   (B) 100 feet   (C) 300 feet   (D) 1,000 feet
5. In this chapter the ship is sailing
   (A) around the tip of South America   (B) across the North
   Sea   (C) in the Indian Ocean   (D) near the Arctic Circle

DRAWING CONCLUSIONS

6. Ned Land and the narrator seem to think the sea monster
   might be
   (A) imaginary   (B) a submarine   (C) a sunken continent
   (D) a reptile

IDENTIFYING THE MOOD

7. Ned Land probably feels that the narrator is
   (A) easygoing and carefree   (B) suspicious and narrow-minded   (C) stubborn and unimaginative   (D) intelligent and easy to talk with

USING YOUR REASON

8. Ned figures that the sea monster is not a fish because a fish would probably NOT
   (A) be so big and clumsy   (B) travel so fast   (C) smell so bad   (D) have steel plates all over

THINKING IT OVER

1. What do the narrator and Ned Land think the monster might be? What arguments do they give? Do you agree with them? Why or why not?

CHAPTER 3

FINDING THE MAIN IDEA

1. The most important thing that happens in this chapter is
   (A) crossing the equator   (B) running out of water
   (C) having a false alarm   (D) finding the monster

REMEMBERING DETAIL

2. The mysterious creature had last been seen in the
   (A) South Pacific   (B) North Pacific   (C) Indian Ocean
   (D) Atlantic Ocean
3. When the "monster" is sighted, the ship has traveled almost to the coast of
   (A) Tahiti   (B) Hawaii   (C) Japan   (D) Australia
4. The prize for seeing the monster first is
   (A) $2,000   (B) $4,000   (C) $10,000   (D) $20,000
5. After the men get restless, the captain gets them to go on for another
   (A) 3 days   (B) 7 days   (C) 10 days   (D) 22 days
6. The excitement of the trip wore off after
   (A) two years   (B) one year   (C) six months
   (D) three months

DRAWING CONCLUSIONS

7. Ned Land is afraid that when he gets home he will
   (A) not have a job   (B) be laughed at   (C) have lost confidence in himself   (D) be sick from lack of vitamins

153

USING YOUR REASON

8. Instead of saying the trip was "a wild goose chase"
Ned Land could have said the trip was
(A) exciting   (B) scary   (C) unsuccessful   (D) wonderful

9. Which is the best reason that Captain Farragut could have
for using Christopher Columbus as an example to his men?
(A) Columbus was a sailor.   (B) Columbus was a brave
man.   (C) Columbus succeeded after almost giving up.
(D) Columbus was rewarded by the king when he returned.

IDENTIFYING THE MOOD

10. In this chapter the mood of the sailors changed from
(A) bored to happy to excited   (B) angry to sad to happy
(C) excited to sad to happy   (D) sad to bored to angry

THINKING IT OVER

1. Ned Land is afraid of what people will say if he returns
without finding the creature. Would you be afraid of being
laughed at if you were Ned? Why or why not?

CHAPTER 4

FINDING THE MAIN IDEA

1. The main thing that happens is that the
(A) monster is caught   (B) captain is killed   (C) ship is
burned   (D) narrator is washed overboard

REMEMBERING DETAIL

2. The monster is described as a
(A) round ball   (B) flat stick   (C) long, pointed oval
(D) fat, hard pyramid

3. How far did the ship chase the monster?
(A) 100 miles   (B) 300 miles   (C) 500 miles   (D) 900
miles

DRAWING CONCLUSIONS

4. The most unusual thing about the creature is that it is
(A) fast   (B) hard   (C) big   (D) electric

USING YOUR REASON

5. The creature is thought to be a whale because it
(A) moved quickly   (B) was strong   (C) was long
(D) spouted steam

IDENTIFYING THE MOOD

6. At the end of the chapter the narrator probably felt
   (A) happy   (B) sad   (C) scared   (D) angry

7. How did the sailors feel all morning?
   (A) bored   (B) excited   (C) cold   (D) lonely

THINKING IT OVER

1. When the ship was flooded, many men were thrown overboard.
   How do you think they felt? How would you have felt?
   Explain your answers.

CHAPTER 5

FINDING THE MAIN IDEA

1. Of the following, the best title for this chapter would be
   (A) "Wounded"   (B) "Lost"   (C) "Captured"
   (D) "Victorious"

REMEMBERING DETAIL

2. What happened to the *Abraham Lincoln?*
   (A) It sank.   (B) It sailed away.   (C) It attacked the
   creature again.   (D) It got caught in a tidal wave.

3. Ned Land and Pierre are almost lost because the submarine
   starts to
   (A) sink   (B) speed away   (C) fire bullets   (D) rise in
   the air

4. The submarine is run by a
   (A) jet of steam   (B) gasoline engine   (C) mechanical
   paddle   (D) screw propeller

USING YOUR REASON

5. Which of the following words is used by Ned Land as a joke?
   (A) Beast   (B) Dive   (C) Sunk   (D) Thing

IDENTIFYING THE MOOD

6. Throughout this chapter Ned Land can be described as
   appearing
   (A) fearful   (B) angry   (C) cheerful   (D) sad

THINKING IT OVER

1. Who do you think the men from the submarine are? What will
   they do to Ned and the professor? Explain your answers.

CHAPTER 6

FINDING THE MAIN IDEA

1. The main problem Ned and the professor have in this chapter is
   (A) keeping warm   (B) finding food   (C) trying to communicate   (D) trying to escape

REMEMBERING DETAIL

2. Ned and Pierre speak to the captain in all of the following languages EXCEPT
   (A) French   (B) Greek   (C) German   (D) Latin
3. Ned and Pierre are in a room lit by
   (A) candles (B) electric lights   (C) gas lights   (D) oil lamps
4. The food on *The Nautilus* is mostly
   (A) fish   (B) seaweed   (C) rice   (D) snails
5. What is unusual about the silverware on *The Nautilus*?
   (A) It is made of gold.   (B) It is delicately carved.   (C) It is made of shell.   (D) It is engraved with a single letter.

IDENTIFYING THE MOOD

6. So far, Ned and Pierre's reactions can be described as
   (A) worried   (B) cautious   (C) angry   (D) afraid

THINKING IT OVER

1. Ned and Pierre were so tired they fell asleep in the submarine. If you were in their place, would you have been able to fall asleep? Why or why not?

CHAPTER 7

FINDING THE MAIN IDEA

1. The most important thing that happens in this chapter is that Ned and Pierre get to
   (A) explore the ship   (B) eat a good meal   (C) talk to the captain   (D) take a look outside

REMEMBERING DETAIL

2. The captain described himself as NOT being
   (A) cultured   (B) intelligent   (C) crazy   (D) civilized

156

3. The captain said that he had the right to
(A) ram other ships   (B) answer no questions   (C) treat Ned and Pierre as enemies   (D) go where he wanted to

DRAWING CONCLUSIONS

4. The captain flatters Pierre by mentioning Pierre's
(A) good looks   (B) book   (C) courage   (D) strong hands
5. Of the following, Pierre seems to place the highest value on
(A) safety   (B) pride   (C) freedom   (D) politeness

USING YOUR REASON

6. The captain did not talk to Ned and Pierre at first because he wanted to
(A) confuse them   (B) think things over   (C) get the ship in order   (D) prepare for an attack
7. The captain can best be compared to the
(A) foreman of a factory   (B) emperor of a nation
(C) scholar in a library   (D) cook in a kitchen
8. What is the captain's relationship with the rest of the world?
(A) He is a spy.   (B) He is on a secret mission for France.
(C) He has left all civilization behind.   (D) He has a plan to attack America.

THINKING IT OVER

1. What does the captain want from Pierre and Ned in return for the freedom of the ship? What would you do if you were in their places? Why?

CHAPTER 8

FINDING THE MAIN IDEA

1. Of the following, the best title for this chapter would be
(A) "Our First Meal in Days"   (B) "Weird Fish and People"   (C) "A Look Around"   (D) "The Captain's Joke"

REMEMBERING DETAIL

2. The cook served something that looked like beef but was really
(A) whale   (B) octopus   (C) seaweed   (D) turtle
3. Which of the following musical instruments is aboard *The Nautilus?*
(A) Piano   (B) Flute   (C) Violin   (D) Organ

4. Pierre says that his cabin was not really a cabin but was rather
   (A) a study   (B) a fine room   (C) a large library
   (D) an apartment
5. Which of the following are the most expensive of Captain Nemo's treasures?
   (A) Rubies   (B) Corals   (C) Pearls   (D) Paintings

DRAWING CONCLUSIONS
6. After seeing the library, Pierre could assume that the captain
   (A) could read several languages   (B) was a skilled painter
   (C) was a mathematician   (D) could read music

USING YOUR REASON
7. The author mentions cigars to show that Captain Nemo
   (A) is rich   (B) makes almost everything from the sea
   (C) uses only the best things   (D) is a good host

IDENTIFYING THE MOOD
8. In this chapter Pierre's mood can best be described as
   (A) despondent   (B) fascinated   (C) scared   (D) angry

THINKING IT OVER
1. If you could have anything you wanted, but you had to stay in a submarine, would you do it? Why or why not?

CHAPTER 9

FINDING THE MAIN IDEA
1. This chapter tells about how
   (A) electricity is made   (B) *The Nautilus* works
   (C) Pierre hears a secret   (D) Ned Land escapes

REMEMBERING DETAIL
2. *The Nautilus* is powered by
   (A) gasoline   (B) sunlight   (C) fish   (C) electricity
3. *The Nautilus* is made mostly of
   (A) aluminum   (B) steel   (C) glass   (D) wood
4. According to Captain Nemo the sub can dive to a depth of
   (A) 20 miles   (B) 15 miles   (C) 9 miles   (D) 6 miles

DRAWING CONCLUSIONS
5. You can assume that Captain Nemo most wants to avoid
   (A) collision with a ship   (B) sinking too deep in the sea
   (C) discovery by the outside world   (D) using up all his wealth

USING YOUR REASON

6. Instead of saying, "I could pay the national debt of France," Captain Nemo would have meant the same thing if he had said:
(A) I have more money than I know what to do with.
(B) Money means nothing to me. (C) Money is the root of all evil. (D) I get money from a very powerful country.

THINKING IT OVER

1. This story takes place over 100 years ago. The author describes many things about *The Nautilus* that we take for granted today, such as electric lights and stoves. What things talked about in this chapter would have seemed very unusual, even fantastic, to Ned and Pierre? How do you think the author could have written about things he had never seen?

CHAPTER 10

FINDING THE MAIN IDEA

1. Another title for this chapter might be
(A) "The Japanese Current" (B) "The Marvels of the Deep" (C) "The Escape Plan" (D) "The Way to Catch Fish"

REMEMBERING DETAIL

2. Ned and Pierre have different attitudes about
(A) staying on the sub (B) where the sub is located
(C) what to eat (D) seeing through the glass
3. Pierre tells Ned to forget about seizing *The Nautilus* because
(A) the ship would explode (B) there are too many sailors
(C) they are lucky to be aboard (D) Captain Nemo is crazy
4. Ned and Pierre decide that they are in the
(A) Gulf Stream (B) Japanese Current (C) Indian Ocean (D) Antarctic
5. Pierre has decided to
(A) escape as soon as possible (B) enjoy the trip
(C) sabotage the ship (D) feel sorry for himself

DRAWING CONCLUSIONS

6. Ned is probably more unhappy than Pierre because Ned is used to

(A) having steak rather than fish   (B) being the captain of his own ship   (C) having things done for him   (D) leading a more active life

IDENTIFYING THE MOOD

7. Ned can be described as being

(A) unhappy   (B) content   (C) angry   (D) lonely

8. Pierre is described as being

(A) anxious   (B) worried   (C) happy   (D) lonely

THINKING IT OVER

1. How would you spend your time if you were on *The Nautilus*? What things would you want with you if you were on *The Nautilus* for a year? Why?

2. Do you think it is really possible for a person to get everything he or she needs from the sea as Captain Nemo claims? What things do you think you could not get from the sea? Explain your answers.

CHAPTER 11

REMEMBERING DETAIL

1. Pierre spends most of his time

(A) walking   (B) sleeping   (C) eating   (D) studying

2. Pierre and Ned received an invitation to

(A) go hunting   (B) hear a concert   (C) enjoy a meal (D) see a play

3. The three men plan to use guns that shoot

(A) tear gas   (B) glass bullets   (C) arrows   (D) darts

4. Crespo Island is a place that has

(A) restaurants   (B) ancient ruins   (C) undersea forests (D) trading stations

DRAWING CONCLUSIONS

5. You can figure out that Nemo gives Ned less respect than he does the professor because he does NOT

(A) invite Ned   (B) give Ned his own invitation

(C) allow Ned to see the ship   (D) give Ned enough to eat

6. Ned is disappointed because he is not going to get to

(A) go outside the sub   (B) escape or eat meat   (C) see the undersea forest   (D) wear a diving suit

USING YOUR REASON

7. The author wrote this chapter to get you ready for a
   (A) change of scene   (B) tragedy   (C) conclusion
   (D) comedy
8. When Nemo says, "There are no hotels on Crespo Island,"
   he really means that it is
   (A) very dangerous   (B) covered with sand   (C) lonely
   and isolated   (D) inhabited by wild animals

THINKING IT OVER

1. What equipment will Ned, Pierre, and the captain use to
   hunt? How do you think it compares to the equipment used
   today? Explain your answers.
2. What do you think the men will be hunting? Describe these
   creatures.

CHAPTER 12

FINDING THE MAIN IDEA

1. This chapter is mostly about
   (A) how diving suits are made   (B) the proper use of guns
   (C) the diver's helmet   (D) exploring undersea life

REMEMBERING DETAIL

2. The underwater suits were made of
   (A) seaweed   (B) rubber   (C) plastic   (D) metal
3. While on the ocean floor, Pierre first notices
   (A) large fish   (B) fine, even sand   (C) the darkness
   (D) the temperature

DRAWING CONCLUSIONS

4. The thick boots probably have lead soles to keep the diver's
   feet
   (A) on the bottom   (B) dry   (C) from getting crushed
   (D) from being bitten by fish

USING YOUR REASON

5. Instead of saying, "I had a feeling of mystery and wonder,"
   Pierre would have meant the same thing if he had said that
   he had a feeling of
   (A) tiredness   (B) fear   (C) awe   (D) depression

CHAPTER 13

REMEMBERING DETAIL

1. Some of the large seaweed reminds Pierre of
   (A) animals   (B) ferns   (C) mountains   (D) birds
2. When confronted with a monster, Captain Nemo
   (A) shoots it   (B) runs from it   (C) hits it
   (D) captures it
3. Captain Nemo shot a
   (A) octopus   (B) sea otter   (C) whale   (D) fish
4. Nemo pushes Ned and Pierre to the ground when they
   (A) hear an explosion   (B) see two sharks   (C) feel
   pressure on their suit   (D) lose air from their suit

DRAWING CONCLUSIONS

5. Ned decides it is useless to try to escape at this time because
   (A) they are too far from civilization   (B) he has no food
   (C) the island is underwater   (D) he is afraid of Captain
   Nemo

USING YOUR REASON

6. When Pierre says, "My blood froze," he would have meant
   the same thing if he had said:
   (A) My hair stood on end.   (B) I fell to the ground.
   (C) My feet got chilled.   (D) My muscles ached.

IDENTIFYING THE MOOD

7. You can tell Ned is happier because he
   (A) jumps up and down   (B) makes funny faces
   (C) sings a song   (D) tells a joke

THINKING IT OVER

1. Ned seems happier in this chapter than he has been since he
   and the professor joined *The Nautilus*. Why do you think he
   is happier now?

CHAPTER 14

FINDING THE MAIN IDEA

1. This chapter is mostly about
   (A) seeing a sunken ship   (B) rescuing some sailors
   (C) passing Hawaii   (D) escaping from sharks

REMEMBERING DETAIL

2. People had tied themselves to the ship to keep
   (A) pirates from attacking   (B) from running aground
   (C) the ship afloat   (D) from being washed overboard
3. According to the professor, Tahiti is the
   (A) newest continent   (B) queen of the Pacific   (C) jewel
   of the West   (D) world's largest coral island

DRAWING CONCLUSIONS

4. The title of this chapter, "Four Thousand Leagues Under the
   Sea," refers to the
   (A) depth of the ocean   (B) amount of time the sub has
   been underwater   (C) length of the journey so far
   (D) number of places the sub has visited

THINKING IT OVER

1. Ned and Pierre assume that the captain is unhappy. They
   wonder if a terrible tragedy might have caused his
   unhappiness. What do you think?
2. The way Christmas is mentioned suggests something about
   the captain's attitude toward life in civilization. What is it?
   Why do you think he feels this way?

CHAPTER 15

FINDING THE MAIN IDEA

1. Another title for this chapter could be
   (A) "The Stewpot of the South Seas"   (B) "The Barrier
   Reef"   (C) "An End to Prison Life"   (D) "Just an
   Incident"

REMEMBERING DETAIL

2. *The Nautilus* is caught on a coral reef that is off the coast of
   (A) Japan   (B) Hawaii   (C) Australia   (D) Tahiti
3. The captain explains that the ship will get off the reef when
   (A) the tide rises   (B) some weight is unloaded   (C) the
   motors are going at full speed   (D) the damage is repaired

DRAWING CONCLUSIONS

4. You can assume that Pierre feels it will be a happy new year
   because for him the trip is
   (A) almost over   (B) very exciting   (C) a big mistake
   (D) very boring

163

5. A full moon is important to Captain Nemo because then
(A) he will be able to work at night   (B) the tide will be the
highest   (C) he can make observations   (D) the damage
will be repaired

USING YOUR REASON

6. The captain allows Ned and Pierre to go ashore mainly
because he
(A) wants some meat   (B) knows they can't escape
(C) wants them out of the way for a while   (D) wonders
what is on the island

IDENTIFYING THE MOOD

7. At the end of the chapter Ned is happy mainly because he
(A) thinks he will escape   (B) has a chance to step outside
the sub   (C) hopes to get some meat to eat   (D) has
decided to accept life on *The Nautilus*

8. When *The Nautilus* is stuck on the reef, Captain Nemo's
attitude is one of
(A) panic   (B) patience   (C) anger   (D) fear

THINKING IT OVER

1. What do you think Ned and Pierre will find on the island?
Give reasons for your answers.

2. Ned and Pierre never managed to learn the language the
captain and his crew spoke. Why do you think this is so?

CHAPTER 16

FINDING THE MAIN IDEA

1. This chapter is mostly about how
(A) Ned and Pierre explore the island   (B) *The Nautilus*
is deserted   (C) breadfruit is cooked   (D) Ned plans to
escape

REMEMBERING DETAIL

2. Breadfruit looks like
(A) small melons   (B) oranges   (C) apples   (D) nuts

3. Ned makes a fire by
(A) using matches   (B) rubbing two sticks together
(C) striking flint and steel   (D) using a magnifying glass

4. Ned and Pierre finish off their meal with
(A) strawberries   (B) nuts   (C) bananas   (D) pineapples

DRAWING CONCLUSIONS

5. The author describes the island as if it were
   (A) a tropical paradise (B) mysterious and strange
   (C) rocky and forbidden (D) a difficult place to live
6. Ned probably considers it reasonable to stay on the island because
   (A) there is plenty of food (B) it is close to civilization
   (C) Captain Nemo has sailed away (D) there is no other choice

IDENTIFYING THE MOOD

7. At the end of the chapter the author creates a sense of
   (A) terror (B) mystery (C) excitement (D) pleasure

THINKING IT OVER

1. What do you think the best course of action for Ned and Pierre to take would be? Why?

CHAPTER 17

FINDING THE MAIN IDEA

1. Another title for this chapter might be
   (A) "A Close Brush With Natives" (B) "Ned is Captured by Indians" (C) "Captain Nemo's Island Paradise"
   (D) "Pierre Saves the Day"

REMEMBERING DETAIL

2. The natives in this chapter are armed with
   (A) knives (B) guns (C) bows and slings (D) spears and swords
3. When Ned and Pierre run aboard *The Nautilus* they find that Captain Nemo
   (A) has disappeared (B) is playing the organ (C) has locked them out (D) is planning an attack
4. *The Nautilus* is protected against attack by
   (A) the dangerous reef (B) guns (C) electricity
   (D) the high tide
5. Pierre figures that the natives had never before seen a
   (A) European (B) large ship (C) submarine
   (D) metal ship

USING YOUR REASON

6. Instead of saying, "I am struck with a thunderbolt!" Ned

would have meant the same thing if he had said:
(A) I have a great idea.   (B) I got a shock.   (C) I've been hit by an arrow.   (D) The gods are with me.
7. Captain Nemo's treatment of the natives shows that he
(A) is prejudiced   (B) is loving and kind   (C) has a cruel nature   (D) does not kill unreasonably

CHAPTER 18

FINDING THE MAIN IDEA

1. The main thing that happens in this chapter is that Ned and Pierre are
(A) locked in chains   (B) drugged   (C) tied with ropes (D) hit over the head

REMEMBERING DETAIL

2. Captain Nemo gets very angry when Pierre
(A) looks through binoculars   (B) disobeys his orders
(C) tells Nemo he wants to leave   (D) refuses to leave the sub
3. The weather during the time that this chapter takes place is
(A) sunny   (B) clear   (C) stormy   (D) snowy

USING YOUR REASON

4. Pierre describes life on *The Nautilus* "like snails" because everyone is
(A) moving very slowly   (B) inside a shell   (C) lost in the ocean   (D) living in a dream
5. You can figure that the events aboard *The Nautilus* have something to do with
(A) the time of day   (B) the weather   (C) the closeness of land   (D) whatever was on the horizon

IDENTIFYING THE MOOD

6. For the first time Captain Nemo seems to show the emotion of
(A) fear   (B) pleasure   (C) excitement   (D) anger

THINKING IT OVER

1. Do you have any idea what Captain Nemo is up to? Do you think Pierre and Ned are in danger for their lives? Why do you think so?

CHAPTER 19

FINDING THE MAIN IDEA

1. Of the following, the best title for this chapter would be
(A) "Mystery of *The Nautilus*"   (B) "An Undersea Burial"
(C) "Equipped for Any Emergency"   (D) "An Immense
Coral Forest"

REMEMBERING DETAIL

2. Nemo said that one of the crew had been wounded by a
(A) falling timber   (B) flying dagger   (C) broken gear
(D) large shark

3. Pierre did not think the captain could
(A) sing   (B) swim   (C) cry   (D) lie

4. The crew aboard *The Nautilus* used the coral forest for
(A) decoration   (B) food   (C) weapons   (D) graves

5. Pierre tells Captain Nemo that he was once a doctor of
(A) biology   (B) medicine   (C) physics   (D) theology

DRAWING CONCLUSIONS

6. You can figure out that Pierre and Ned are allowed the
freedom of the sub again because
(A) Nemo now trusts them   (B) they promised not to
escape   (C) whatever Nemo was hiding is gone   (D) Nemo
needs their help to run the sub

IDENTIFYING THE MOOD

7. The last sentence of the chapter indicates that Captain Nemo
has bad feelings about
(A) people   (B) Pierre   (C) the sea   (D) coral

THINKING IT OVER

1. How does Captain Nemo feel about the men in his crew?
How are his feelings shown? Do you think the captain is
sincere? Why or why not?

PART II

CHAPTER 1

REMEMBERING DETAIL

1. The sharks that followed *The Nautilus* were
   (A) 18 feet long   (B) 25 feet long   (C) 28 feet long
   (D) 35 feet long
2. The island of Ceylon is noted for its
   (A) whaling   (B) sugar cane   (C) pearl fishing   (D) oil
3. Captain Nemo says that one of the thrills of pearl fishing is
   (A) swimming   (B) sharks   (C) octopuses   (D) diving
4. Pearls vary in price according to size, polish, and
   (A) weight   (B) smoothness   (C) color   (D) hardness
5. Pearls are made by
   (A) sharks   (B) oysters   (C) fish   (D) people

DRAWING CONCLUSIONS

6. You can figure that Ned and Pierre are eager to go with
   Captain Nemo because they are
   (A) bored   (B) hungry   (C) greedy   (D) afraid

USING YOUR REASON

7. According to Pierre, Captain Nemo might be trying to
   (A) discover a new continent   (B) become rich   (C) get
   even with the world   (D) lose touch with other people

THINKING IT OVER

1. Do you think the captain hates the world? Or do you think
   that he has a reason for what he is doing? Explain your
   answers.

CHAPTER 2

FINDING THE MAIN IDEA

1. This chapter is mostly about how
   (A) Pierre steals a pearl   (B) Ned is attacked
   (C) Captain Nemo fights a shark   (C) a diver drowns
2. The title that tells the most about this chapter is
   (A) "Life Under the Sea"   (B) "A Large Pearl"
   (C) "Fight with a Shark"   (D) "King of the Sea"

168

REMEMBERING DETAIL

3. The large oyster weighed about
   (A) 35 pounds (B) 200 pounds (C) 500 pounds
   (D) 750 pounds
4. The shark is finally killed when
   (A) Nemo stabs it (B) Ned harpoons it (C) Pierre
   shoots it (D) other sharks attack it
5. Nemo gave the fisherman some
   (A) oysters (B) harpoons (C) money (D) pearls
6. The shark was large and measured about
   (A) 25 feet (B) 15 feet (C) 10 feet (D) 8 feet

USING YOUR REASON

7. Instead of saying, "I was nailed to the spot," Pierre would
   have meant the same thing if he had said:
   (A) I was struck with a knife. (B) My boots were caught
   on the bottom. (C) I was scared stiff. (D) I fought like
   a tiger.

THINKING IT OVER

1. Captain Nemo says that he is one of the oppressed. What does
   he mean by that? Do you think he really feels that way?
   Explain your answers.
2. How do you think the fisherman felt when he saw the three
   men in their diving suits? How would you have felt? Explain
   your answers.

CHAPTER 3

FINDING THE MAIN IDEA

1. The main thing that happens in this chapter is that Captain
   Nemo explains how he
   (A) got so rich (B) loves the sea (C) gets through the
   Isthmus of Suez (D) plans to own the world

REMEMBERING DETAIL

2. Since the beginning of the story, *The Nautilus* has traveled
   about
   (A) 5,000 miles (B) 11,000 miles (C) 16,000 miles
   (D) 27,000 miles

3. Captain Nemo discovered an underground tunnel by
(A) using electronic equipment   (B) putting rings around
fish   (C) putting dye in the water   (D) dropping weights
into the sea
4. According to the captain, the Red Sea got its name from the
(A) many people who died there   (B) the microscopic
plants   (C) beautiful sunsets that can be seen   (D) color
of the sand

USING YOUR REASON
5. You can figure out that this story was written a long time
ago because the
(A) Red Sea has dried up   (B) Arabian Tunnel is used all
the time   (C) sponges Pierre saw are all extinct   (D) Suez
Canal had not yet been dug
6. Pierre talks about Moses and the Egyptians because he
(A) is a captive like Moses was   (B) plans to escape like
Moses did   (C) is visiting the location where Moses escaped
(D) wonders if the story of Moses is true

IDENTIFYING THE MOOD
7. When Pierre finds out how the captain plans to get to the
Mediterranean Sea, he feels
(A) surprised   (B) afraid   (C) indifferent   (D) worried

CHAPTER 4

FINDING THE MAIN IDEA
1. The title that tells the most about this chapter is
(A) "Mount Sinai"   (B) "The Pilot's Cage"   (C) "The
Undersea Tunnel"   (D) "Walls of Coral"

REMEMBERING DETAIL
2. Who steered *The Nautilus* in this chapter?
(A) Pierre   (B) the navigator   (C) Ned   (D) Nemo
3. The pilot's cage reminded Pierre of a
(A) prison   (B) steamboat   (C) tree house   (D) bubble
4. How long did it take *The Nautilus* to get from the Red Sea
to the Mediterranean?
(A) five minutes   (B) ten minutes   (C) thirty minutes
(D) forty-five minutes
5. The strange roaring that Pierre heard was made by the

(A) water   (B) engine   (C) rocks   (D) air pressure
6. According to the chapter, the Mediterranean has a lower sea
   level than the
   (A) Pacific Ocean   (B) Indian Ocean   (C) Atlantic Ocean
   (D) Red Sea
7. You can figure that Pierre found the trip through the tunnel
   to be
   (A) frightening   (B) thrilling   (C) boring   (D) peaceful

CHAPTER 5

FINDING THE MAIN IDEA
1. The title that tells the most about this chapter is
   (A) "The Control Room"   (B) "An Undersea Walk"
   (C) "The Mystery of the Gold"   (D) "A Dark Night"

REMEMBERING DETAIL
2. Pierre wants to stay on *The Nautilus* mostly because he
   (A) likes it better than land   (B) is afraid to leave
   (C) wants to finish his book   (D) admires Captain Nemo
3. Pierre agrees with Ned that their escape should occur
   (A) in a few months   (B) in a few days   (C) at the first
   opportunity   (D) only after careful consideration
4. The diver that approached *The Nautilus* carried a
   (A) sack of gold   (B) leather bag   (C) gold knife
   (D) wooden chest
5. Captain Nemo's iron chest is filled with
   (A) pearls   (B) diamonds   (C) gold   (D) jewelry

DRAWING CONCLUSIONS
6. You can figure out the nationality of the diver because of the
   (A) way he looked   (B) language Nemo wrote the address
   in   (C) location of *The Nautilus*   (D) kind of job he has

USING YOUR REASON
7. Which of the following questions is left unanswered?
   (A) Who is the diver?   (B) Who received the gold?
   (C) Where is *The Nautilus* located?   (D) What was in the
   chest?

IDENTIFYING THE MOOD
8. Pierre's mood can be described best as being
   (A) solemn   (B) sad   (C) curious   (D) anxious

1. It is obvious that Captain Nemo is very rich. Would you like to be very rich? What would you do if you were rich? Where would you live? How would you spend your time?

CHAPTER 6

FINDING THE MAIN IDEA

1. The main purpose of this chapter is to
(A) tell about Nemo's wealth and how he uses it   (B) tell where to find sunken treasure and how to get it   (C) show how Ned will eventually escape   (D) explain how Spanish ships were sunk

REMEMBERING DETAIL

2. Ned and Pierre delayed their plans for escape mostly because they were
(A) too close to land   (B) lost at sea   (C) afraid of the captain   (D) traveling too fast and deep

3. Captain Nemo says that he gets his wealth mostly from
(A) mines under the ocean   (B) pearl fishing   (C) sunken treasure   (D) undersea mines

4. The wealth that Captain Nemo gathers is used largely for
(A) inventions   (B) charity   (C) war   (D) travel

5. What takes place at Vigo Bay?
(A) Pierre discovers gold.   (B) Captain Nemo finds pearls.
(C) Ned tries to escape.   (D) Sailors recover sunken treasure.

DRAWING CONCLUSIONS

6. You can figure that in order to leave the Mediterranean *The Nautilus* would have to travel in which direction?
(A) north   (B) south   (C) east   (D) west

USING YOUR REASON

7. Pierre figures that Captain Nemo dislikes the Mediterranean because Captain Nemo
(A) dumps garbage in it   (B) says that he hates it   (C) is in a hurry to leave it   (D) hides in his cabin

IDENTIFYING THE MOOD

8. Upon arriving in Vigo Bay, Captain Nemo feels
(A) sad   (B) cheerful   (C) frantic   (D) angry

1. Have you ever thought of searching for buried treasure? What would you do with it if you found it? Tell why.

CHAPTER 7

FINDING THE MAIN IDEA

1. The author's main purpose in this chapter is to show Ned's
   (A) sense of humor   (B) interest in the sea   (C) growing rage at his imprisonment   (D) skill as a harpooner

REMEMBERING DETAIL

2. Pierre explains which of the following to Ned?
   (A) The ways of fish   (B) The nature of the Gulf Stream
   (C) The feeding habits of sharks   (D) The reason for fog

3. *The Nautilus* visits a "quiet place" in the ocean that is called the
   (A) Gulf of Mexico   (B) South Pole   (C) Equator
   (D) Saragasso Sea

4. *The Nautilus* travels across the sea at the rate of
   (A) 20 miles per day   (B) 40 miles per day   (C) 300 miles per day   (D) 500 miles per day

5. Pierre thinks that there is enough air in *The Nautilus* for one day for how many persons?
   (A) 30   (B) 67   (C) 340   (D) 625

6. At the end of the chapter *The Nautilus* has sailed to the
   (A) Indian Ocean   (B) Adriatic Sea   (C) South Atlantic
   (D) North Pacific

USING YOUR REASON

7. When Pierre refers to Captain Nemo's "undersea bank" he is talking about
   (A) valuable fish   (B) a tunnel   (C) sunken treasure
   (D) *The Nautilus*

8. Pierre says that it would be "madness indeed" for Captain Nemo to go to
   (A) New York   (B) the Saragasso   (C) Atlantis   (D) the South Pole

THINKING IT OVER

1. At the end of this chapter we seem to be left with the

question, "Where are we headed next?" Where do you think *The Nautilus* is headed? Why do you think so?
2. What is Ned's character like? Why is he getting so angry? What would you do if you were in his place?

CHAPTER 8

FINDING THE MAIN IDEA
1. The main thing that happens in this chapter is that *The Nautilus*
(A) arrives at the South Pole   (B) dives deeper than ever before   (C) sinks under the ice   (D) gets stuck in the ice

REMEMBERING DETAIL
2. *The Nautilus* is heated by
(A) sunlight   (B) steam heat   (C) wood stoves
(D) electric heaters
3. While outside the sub, men wear
(A) wool sweaters   (B) polar bear fur suits   (C) insulated rubber suits   (D) leather jackets
4. The biggest problem in getting to the South Pole, according to Captain Nemo, will involve the supply of
(A) power   (B) heat   (C) air   (D) food

DRAWING CONCLUSIONS
5. You can figure that Captain Nemo is going to the South Pole in order to
(A) get something he has left there   (B) find a safe place to hide   (C) be the first person to do so   (D) discover new forms of life

USING YOUR REASON
6. Ned and Pierre think that *The Nautilus* will be stuck in the ice for a long time because
(A) winter is too near for the ice to break up   (B) no other ship will help them get out   (C) *The Nautilus* has lost its source of power   (D) Captain Nemo has lost his will to go on
7. At the end of the chapter Captain Nemo is
(A) complaining   (B) satisfied   (C) sorry   (D) lonely

174

CHAPTER 9

FINDING THE MAIN IDEA

1. The best title for the chapter would be
   (A) "The Seals of the South Pole"   (B) "Captain Nemo
   Watches the Stars"   (C) "Under the South Pole"
   (D) "The Discovery of the South Pole"

REMEMBERING DETAIL

2. All of the following animals are mentioned as being at the
   South Pole EXCEPT
   (A) albatrosses   (B) seals   (C) ducks   (D) penguins
3. The exporers could not take their position by the sun for two
   days because the sun was
   (A) below the horizon   (B) too high in the sky
   (C) hidden by fog   (D) behind the mountains
4. When did Captain Nemo claim the South Pole?
   (A) June 1, 1787   (B) May 20, 1823   (C) October 15,
   1843   (D) March 21, 1868
5. Captain Nemo marked the South Pole with a
   (A) monument   (B) stick   (C) flag   (D) dye

DRAWING CONCLUSIONS

6. You can figure that Captain Nemo has a grudge against
   people when he says:
   (A) "In my own, sir."   (B) "Good-by, proud sun."
   (C) "You are right, it is tomorrow or never."   (D) "No
   person has ever been here before me."
7. You can figure that a chronometer is a kind of
   (A) speedometer   (B) clock   (C) depth gauge
   (D) barometer

IDENTIFYING THE MOOD

8. At the end of the chapter Captain Nemo appears to be
   (A) angry   (B) satisfied   (C) disagreeable   (D) disgusted

THINKING IT OVER

1. The South Pole was really discovered in 1911 by a Norwegian
   explorer, Roald Amundsen. Do you think Amundsen found
   the Pole to be like the description in this chapter? Explain
   your answer.

CHAPTER 10

FINDING THE MAIN IDEA
1. The main thing that happens to *The Nautilus* in this chapter is that it
   (A) springs a leak   (B) runs aground   (C) is trapped under the ice   (D) is frozen into an iceberg

REMEMBERING DETAIL
2. *The Nautilus* is in trouble because of
   (A) weather   (B) ice   (C) animals   (D) men
3. The tunnel is how wide?
   (A) Five yards   (B) Ten yards   (C) Twenty yards
   (D) Fifty yards
4. Pierre found that the pictures hanging on the wall
   (A) fell to the ground   (B) broke into pieces   (C) hung straight out   (D) floated on the ceiling

USING YOUR REASON
5. Instead of saying that *The Nautilus* is "stranded," it would mean the same thing to say that it is
   (A) stuck   (B) lost   (C) broken   (D) abandoned

IDENTIFYING THE MOOD
6. The mood of the people aboard *The Nautilus* is
   (A) sad   (B) worried   (C) angry   (D) cheerful

THINKING IT OVER
1. According to Nemo, there is a difference between an "accident" and an "incident." What do you think the difference is?

CHAPTER 11

FINDING THE MAIN IDEA
1. The main thing that happens in this chapter is that the men
   (A) view the sea bottom   (B) escape from an ice prison
   (C) wait for the ice to melt   (D) work without stopping

REMEMBERING DETAIL
2. Ned says he is as handy with a pickax as he is with a
   (A) fork   (B) harpoon   (C) gun   (D) shovel

176

3. The air reservoir held enough air for how many days?
   (A) 1   (B) 2   (C) 4   (D) 8
4. The men wear jackets made of
   (A) wool   (B) leather   (C) rubber   (D) cork
5. Pierre prefers to work rather than rest because
   (A) it gives him hope   (B) the air is better   (C) he needs
   the exercise   (D) he is afraid to be alone

DRAWING CONCLUSIONS
6. The men on *The Nautilus* show courage mostly by
   (A) continuing to work   (B) singing and shouting
   (C) obeying every order   (D) sharing what they have
7. In this chapter, Pierre is almost
   (A) drowned   (B) hanged   (C) suffocated   (D) stabbed

IDENTIFYING THE MOOD
8. Pierre's feelings during most of this chapter could best be
   described as
   (A) angry   (B) bitter   (C) hateful   (D) scared

THINKING IT OVER
1. How do you think the men aboard *The Nautilus* felt while
   they were caught in the ice? How would you have felt in their
   place? What would you have done?

CHAPTER 12

FINDING THE MAIN IDEA
1. The best title for this chapter would be
   (A) "Lost at Sea"   (B) "Speeding Across the Atlantic"
   (C) "Killing Time at Sea"   (D) "Fishing for Sea Cows"

REMEMBERING DETAIL
2. The men were filled with delight by
   (A) the stars   (B) fresh air   (C) food   (D) the sea
3. Instead of thinking about the South Pole, Pierre and Ned start
   to think of
   (A) the sea   (B) animals   (C) escape   (D) home
4. In this chapter Captain Nemo
   (A) remains below deck   (B) issues new commands
   (C) takes Pierre ashore   (D) makes a discovery

5. Ned talked of escaping near French Guiana but does not because it was too
(A) windy   (B) foggy   (C) hot   (D) cold

DRAWING CONCLUSIONS

6. You can figure that Tierra del Fuego probably means
(A) Land of Plenty   (B) Land of Savages   (C) Land of Smoke   (D) Land of Fish
7. Pierre delivers a little talk on the subject of
(A) astronomy   (B) ecology   (C) medicine
(D) algebra

THINKING IT OVER

1. What do you think the author meant by the term "balance of nature" as it is used in this chapter?

CHAPTER 13

FINDING THE MAIN IDEA

1. The main thing that happens in this chapter is that the men of *The Nautilus*
(A) fight giant octopuses   (B) chase an octopus
(C) catch a large octopus   (D) see a huge octopus

REMEMBERING DETAIL

2. Ned said he saw a ship pulled into the sea by an octopus in
(A) the Pacific   (B) a movie   (C) Mexico   (D) his hometown
3. Pierre fights the octopus using
(A) a gun   (B) an ax   (C) a harpoon   (D) a knife
4. The octopus escapes by
(A) hiding behind the captain   (B) getting lost in the sand
(C) blinding the men   (D) killing all the men

DRAWING CONCLUSIONS

5. The dying sailor's last cries bother Pierre because he
(A) almost saved the sailor   (B) was almost the one to die
(C) knew the sailor as a friend   (D) heard them in his native language
6. You can figure that *The Nautilus* drifts aimlessly because Captain Nemo
(A) has been wounded   (B) is undecided about where to go

(C) is grieving for his lost crew member   (D) has left the
ship to go ashore

THINKING IT OVER

1. Earlier in the story we saw how *The Nautilus* was electrified.
This stopped attackers from coming aboard. Why do you
think *The Nautilus* was not electrified to fight off the
octopuses? Explain your answer.

CHAPTER 14

FINDING THE MAIN IDEA

1. The title that tells the most about this chapter is
(A) "How Hurricanes Grow"   (B) "*The Nautilus* Rides a
Hurricane"   (C) "*The Nautilus* Turns Back"   (D) "*The
Nautilus* Sinks Below the Waves"

REMEMBERING DETAIL

2. Ned says that he would rather die than go past
(A) Long Island   (B) Boston   (C) the St. Lawrence
(D) Newfoundland

3. Ned and Pierre have now been on *The Nautilus* for how
many months?
(A) 7   (B) 9   (C) 12   (D) 16

4. The hurricane occurs when *The Nautilus* is closest to
(A) the Bahamas   (B) Long Island   (C) Cape Hatteras
(D) Nova Scotia

DRAWING CONCLUSIONS

5. At the end of the chapter Pierre is "crushed and weak"
because he
(A) is afraid of the storm   (B) is unable to leave *The
Nautilus*   (C) has been outside in the storm   (D) has been
unable to sleep

6. You can figure that Pierre is now ready to leave *The Nautilus*
because he
(A) finally realizes that Captain Nemo is dangerous
(B) has completed his book   (C) is afraid of further
adventures   (D) worries about Ned's health

THINKING IT OVER

1. Why does Pierre consider Captain Nemo "admirable," despite

the captain's unfriendly attitude? Do you think Captain Nemo is admirable? Why do you think that?

CHAPTER 15

FINDING THE MAIN IDEA

1. The main thing that happens in this chapter is that *The Nautilus*
(A) destroys a ship   (B) captures the enemy   (C) is overturned   (D) is recognized by a passing ship

REMEMBERING DETAIL

2. Cyrus Field is mentioned as the man who
(A) financed the Atlantic cable   (B) discovered *The Nautilus*   (C) explored the North Sea   (D) bears Captain Nemo a grudge
3. Ned Land hopes that a warship will sink *The Nautilus* because he
(A) hates Captain Nemo   (B) thinks he will be able to escape   (C) feels *The Nautilus* is a danger to mankind (D) has decided to die rather than continue as a prisoner
4. Captain Nemo threatens to kill Ned when Ned
(A) strikes Captain Nemo   (B) talks back to Captain Nemo   (C) tries to signal the ship   (D) tries to escape in the dinghy
5. Pierre watches the ship sink from a point
(A) in his room   (B) on deck   (C) in the dining room (D) in front of the glass panel

DRAWING CONCLUSIONS

6. You can figure that Captain Nemo's personal problems have something to do with his
(A) mother   (B) wife and children   (C) country (D) occupation

IDENTIFYING THE MOOD

7. When Pierre sees the ship and men sinking, his mood is one of
(A) despair   (B) fright   (C) anger   (D) depression
8. Captain Nemo's mood changes in this chapter from
(A) joy to sadness   (B) hate to grief   (C) love to hate (D) sorrow to anger

THINKING IT OVER

1. How would you have felt if you had been aboard *The Nautilus* when it sank the ship? What would you have done? Explain your answers.

CHAPTER 16

FINDING THE MAIN IDEA

1. The title that tells most about this chapter is
(A) "Nemo Sees a Ghost"   (B) "Escape into the Maelstrom"   (B) "Bad Weather"   (D) "An Easy Escape"

REMEMBERING DETAIL

2. Ned and Pierre decide to escape and row to land that is how many miles away?
(A) two   (B) six   (C) ten   (D) twenty

3. Pierre takes the notes for his book and puts them in
(A) a sack   (B) the inside pockets of his coat   (C) a waterproof case   (D) a box in the boat

4. The Maelstrom is a kind of
(A) storm   (B) rock   (C) whirlpool   (D) monster

5. The last words of Captain Nemo are:
(A) "Free at last!"   (B) "Enough! Enough!"   (C) "It's mine forever!"   (D) "Farewell, sweet ocean!"

DRAWING CONCLUSIONS

7. You can figure from Captain Nemo's behavior in this chapter that he is
(A) afraid to die   (B) no longer sane   (C) glad to be alive
(D) trying to remember something

IDENTIFYING THE MOOD

8. As the dinghy breaks loose from *The Nautilus,* Pierre's mood might best be described as
(A) joyful   (B) sad   (C) fearful   (D) angry

THINKING IT OVER

1. What do you think Captain Nemo's last words meant?

FINDING THE MAIN IDEA

1. The best title for this chapter would be
   (A) "The Mysterious Island"   (B) "The Fishing Village"
   (C) "Safe at Last"   (D) "Home at Last"

REMEMBERING DETAIL

2. Pierre wakes up to find that he is in a
   (A) hospital   (B) ship   (C) town house   (D) fisherman's hut

3. Pierre and Ned are in the Lofoten Islands, near
   (A) Norway   (B) England   (C) America   (D) Italy

4. How often does a steamship visit the Lofoten Islands?
   (A) Once a week   (B) Once every two weeks   (C) Once a month   (D) Once a year

5. Ned and Pierre plan to go to
   (A) Scotland   (B) France   (C) America   (D) Spain

6. Pierre hopes that Captain Nemo is
   (A) at peace   (B) dead   (C) captured   (D) gone forever

THINKING IT OVER

1. What do you think happened to Captain Nemo and *The Nautilus?* Explain your answer.